Secret o

UFOs from inside the Earth

Brinsley Le Poer Trench

Secret of the Ages

UFOs from inside the Earth

Panther

Granada Publishing Limited
Published in 1976 by Panther Books Ltd
Frogmore, St Albans, Herts AL2 2NF
Reprinted 1976

First published in Great Britain by
Souvenir Press Ltd 1974
Copyright © 1974 by Brinsley Le Poer Trench
Made and printed in Great Britain by
Richard Clay (The Chaucer Press) Ltd
Bungay, Suffolk
Set in Linotype Times

To MILDRED

This book is dedicated to my dear friend, Mildred Alleyn Spong, who for over a quarter of a century has been a source of inspiration and joy to me.

Contents

Illustrations

Alice laughed. 'There's no use trying,' she said, 'one can't believe impossible things.'

'I daresay you haven't had much practice,' said the Queen. 'When I was younger, I always did it for half an hour a day. Why, sometimes I've believed as many as six impossible things before breakfast.'

LEWIS CARROLL
Through the Looking Glass

Acknowledgments

I wish to thank Mr. Raymond A. Palmer, editor and publisher of *Flying Saucers*, for his kind permission to quote extensively and for supplying considerable source material including the satellite photographs which are reproduced from his magazine.

Acknowledgments are made to the Environmental Science Service Administration, U.S. Department of Commerce, for the ESSA-3 and ESSA-7 pictures, and to the National Aeronautics and Space Administration (NASA) for the two photographs taken by the ATS-111 camera, reproduced from the NASA book *Exploring Space with a Camera*.

I would also like to thank Mr. J. B. Delair, editor of the Contact International (U.K.) publication, *The UFO Register*, for providing extensive source material and valuable advice for the Atlantis section of this book.

Mr. Charles Bowen, editor of *Flying Saucer Review*, for his kind permission to quote extensively.

Miss Anthea Smith and Mr. Sean Wellband for specialized assistance.

The undermentioned publishers for permission to quote material from the books listed:

The author and Turnstone Books, London. *Maps of the Ancient Sea Kings: Evidence of Advanced Civilization in the Ice Age*, by Charles H. Hapgood, 1975. Also published in the U.S.A. by Chilton Books, Philadelphia.

Arco Publications Ltd., London, and Citadel Press, Secaucus, N. J. *Flying Saucers Uncensored*, by Harold T. Wilkins, 1955.

Faber & Faber Ltd., London. *Moons, Myths and Man: A Reinterpretation*, 1936, and, *Built Before the Flood: The Problem of the Tiahuanaco Ruins*, 1947, both by H. S. Bellamy.

Garnstone Press, London. *Timeless Earth*, by Peter Kolosimo, 1973.

George G. Harrap & Co. Ltd., London. *The Myths of Greece and Rome*, by H. A. Guerber, 1953.

Health Research, Box 70, Mokelumne Hill, California, 95245, U.S.A. *The Phantom of the Poles*, by William Reed, 1964 (originally published by Walter S. Rockey Company, New York, 1906), and, *A Journey to the Earth's Interior – or Have the Poles really been Discovered?* by Marshall B. Gardner, 1964 (originally published by the author at Aurora, Illinois, 1920).

Rider and Company, London (A member of the Hutchinson Publishing Group). *The Shadow of Atlantis*, by Colonel A. Braghine, 1938. *The Riddle of the Earth*, by Comyns Beaumont (writing under the pseudonym of Appian Way), 1924. *The History of Atlantis*, 1925, and, *The Problem of Atlantis*, 1925, both by Lewis Spence. *Mysteries of Ancient South America*, 1946, and, *Secret Cities of Old South America*, 1950, both by Harold T. Wilkins.

Souvenir Press, London. *The Gold of the Gods*, by Erich von Daniken, 1973.

Finally, I would like to thank the editors of the following magazine and newspapers:

Saga Magazine, U.S.A. Permission to quote from the article 'The UFO Evidence Everyone Ignores', by John A. Keel, in their June, 1973, issue.

The Sunday Express. Permission to quote from a news story by Penny Hart entitled 'Victim of the ghostly hum pays £2,000 to trace it!' in their issue of 18 June, 1972.

The Times. Permission to reprint the news story 'Puma is seen stalking a rabbit' from their issue of 6 July, 1966;

and

a special word of thanks to Mr. Egerton Sykes who kindly provided data on traces of Atlantean cities under the Atlantic Ocean as this book was about to go to press, which I was delighted to incorporate.

Introduction

Anyone who puts forward an idea that is contrary to all accepted scientific views and to long established beliefs is a suitable target for ridicule. However, much more eminent people than myself over the centuries have received the full treatment of scorn and derision. Often though, their ideas and discoveries eventually have been vindicated and proved correct. Galileo Galilei is an example from the past and Immanuel Velikovsky in our own times.

In this book it is proposed to present first a case for the reality of Atlantis – the lost continent. Many other writers have tried to do this before me, but it is an essential part of my case for the hollow Earth that follows. Possibly, I will produce some data and hitherto unknown information about Atlantis. I firmly believe that Atlantis existed and am confident that my researches will convince you of its reality.

Secondly, I will be presenting proof for the Earth being hollow with entrances into the interior from both the north and south polar areas. Other smaller entrances scattered about the Earth's surface leading into great tunnel systems connecting with the cavern world inside the Earth will be mentioned.

The Ancients built these great tunnel systems, and as you will see in the first part of this book, they lived both inside and on the surface of the Earth. You see, our planet, like all others, is really a great spaceship sailing through the ocean of Space. Inside our ship are myriads of passages, vast halls and even great cities! We are just living on the deck of our ship unaware of all the life and activity going on, literally under our feet. This is now the most closely guarded international secret of the ages.

Thirdly, based on the conviction that a hollow Earth really exists, reasons will be produced to suggest that a large proportion of the unidentified flying objects (UFOs), more popularly known as 'flying saucers', emanate from the Earth's interior.

Now, it must be admitted that in one of my earlier books scorn was poured on the hollow Earth theory then believed in by a minority of ufologists.[1]* You see, I had been educated along with millions of other people to believe that the Earth had a liquid molten core. This is no longer accepted scientific thinking. Once this fact became known to me, I read and researched deeply into this fascinating subject, and came to the conclusion that the Earth was really hollow.

It always takes courage to amend your views, especially when they have been expressed publicly in print. We should all be adaptable to new ideas, and if the evidence is there, not be afraid to bring it forward, even if it runs contrary to what we have previously written.

The contents of this book do not contradict anything in my previous ones, with the above exception. I still firmly consider that some of the UFOs come from other worlds in our physical universe and some from invisible ones, in another order of matter, too. Some, too, may come from bases under the sea, an idea proposed by the late Ivan T. Sanderson in his remarkable book *Invisible Residents*.[2]

It should also be stated that the hollow Earth theory did not originate in my little grey cells. Several books were written shortly after the turn of the century advocating this idea, notably two by Marshall B. Gardner[3] and William Reed.[4]

A lot of the questions that both Gardner and Reed asked have still not been answered. The questions raised by these two learned gentlemen, coupled with more modern evidence and satellite photographs of the polar areas, will be

* The numbers in the text refer to the References at the end of the book.

the main basis of my argument for a hollow Earth.

However, as a curtain raiser, we are first going to have a look at the legendary Atlantis – and this has a lot to do with the hollow Earth – and this author hopes to prove to you that Atlantis was not just a legend but a reality.

Part One   The Case for Atlantis

1: The Location of Atlantis

Thousands of books have been written in many languages about the lost continent of Atlantis. Indeed, according to Colonel A. Braghine, writing in *The Shadow of Atlantis*, there are more than 25,000 volumes dedicated to Atlantology alone in one library in Paris. Incidentally, Braghine's book was published in 1938, so there may be quite a few more by now![1]

Plato has preserved for mankind a history of Atlantis in his *Dialogues: Timaeus* and *Critias*. However, as these were regarded as examples of his more popular rather than serious works, his narrative about the sinking of Atlantis has been regarded as a fable by many critics.

Nevertheless, there are so many similarities on both sides of the Atlantic Ocean, in regard to sun worship, pyramid building, symbols and hieroglyphics on rocks, semantics, culture, arts and traditions, that when studying the whole question of Atlantis in depth, you are left with no choice but to accept that there was once such a tremendous civilization which was obliterated in a great catastrophe or a series of catastrophes. That is, unless you are the most hardened sceptic with a built-in mechanism that won't allow you to believe in something until it is actually before your eyes.

Ignatius Donnelly in his comprehensive and scholarly work, *Atlantis: The Antediluvian World*, commented upon that type of person in these words:

The fact the story of Atlantis was for thousands of years regarded as a fable proves nothing. There is an unbelief which grows out of ignorance, as well as a scepticism which is born of intelligence. The people nearest to the past are not always those who are best informed concerning the past.

For a thousand years it was believed that the legends of the buried cities of Pompeii and the Herculaneum were myths: they were spoken of as 'the fabulous cities'.

For a thousand years the educated world did not credit the accounts given by Herodotus of the wonders of the ancient civilizations of the Nile and Chaldea. He was called 'the father of Liars'. Even Plutarch sneered at him. Now, in the language of Frederick Schlegel, 'the deeper and more comprehensive the researches of the moderns have been, the more their regard and esteem for Herodotus has increased'. Buckle says, 'His minute information about Egypt and Asia Minor is admitted by all geographers."[2]

Another more recent example that can be given is the discovery made by an amateur archaeologist, Dr. Heinrich Schliemann. He unearthed his Troy which few people believed to have existed.

If we go back to the furthest historical and traditional records of the human race, the conclusion is reached that in exceedingly ancient times civilization, culture, art, commerce and colonization were originated and, subsequently, maintained by a mysterious race of white and bearded men of fair complexion who evidently held sway over most of the earth, but of whom history preserves few definite traces. The veil of time has descended and almost obliterated their memory; yet they, and the vast complex culture they created, did exist.

Evidence supporting and confirming this is surprisingly abundant if you know how and where to locate it. The sources include the traditions, folklore and early literature of many nations, both in the New World and in the Old, and sculptured edifices of great age.

Where was Atlantis situated? That is a question that has puzzled Atlantologists for centuries. Many theories have been put forward. The Atlantean associations with certain special areas and specific monumental edifices have been pretty certainly established, and it is now possible to trace their activities in many parts of the world. It is a most remarkable fact, however, that the greatest or most abundant traces of this ancient white race occur in the lands surrounding the Atlantic Ocean – especially in South America – in the Andean region of Peru, Bolivia and Colombia. The main focal centre of their culture seems, from many points of view, to have been located somewhere between West Africa and Brazil, or eastwards of the West Indies.

It is obviously of fundamental importance to prove or disprove the existence of these long vanished lands, since the possibility of their former existence would, if irrevocably established, clearly alter our conception of the origin and antiquity of civilization.

The following material seems to support the belief that in the comparatively very recent past (geologically speaking) there existed a large land mass, or several land bridges connecting the present transatlantic continents in the Atlantic Ocean, and that these lands foundered through a great natural upheaval well within the 'Human Period'.

The story of Atlantis, first popularized by Plato, has attracted the attention of many serious-minded scholars down the ages since Greek and Roman times. The conclusions reached by writers upon this subject are most diverse. Some staunchly supported the hypothesis (amply proved by geological and palaeontological testimony) that a very real Atlantean continent existed until comparatively recent times; others, ridiculing that idea, advanced counterarguments disproving – in their estimation – the recent existence of any extensive land mass in the Atlantic. The available evidence, however, when reviewed dispassionately, undoubtedly confirms the former and the very recent existence in the Atlantic of one or more land masses.

Dr. Lewis Spence ably surveyed earlier notions about the lost continent in his book, *The Problem of Atlantis*.

Many of the older geologists were in favour of the idea of an Atlantean continent. Lyell confessed to its likelihood, though he could not see in the Atlantic islands traces of a mid-Atlantic ridge. [This, of course, has now been found.] Buffon dated the separation of the New and Old Worlds from the catastrophe of Atlantis. In 1846 Forbes declared his belief in the former existence of a bridge of islands in the North Atlantic, and in 1856 Heer attempted to show the necessity of a similar connection from the testimony of palaeontological history. In 1860 Unger tried to explain the likeness between the fossil flora of Europe and the living flora of Asia by virtue of the Atlantean hypothesis, and Kuntze, who was struck with the case of the tropical seedless banana occurring at once in Asia and in America before the discovery of the latter continent (by Columbus), saw in this a strange evidence of the truth of the Atlantean theory.[3]

Professor E. Hull, in *The Sub-Oceanic Physiography of the North Atlantic*, wrote:

The flora and fauna of the two hemispheres support the geological theory that there was a common centre in the Atlantic, where organic life began, and that prior to the glacial epoch great land bridges north and south spanned the Atlantic Ocean.[4]

French geologists have for some unknown reason always been positively sympathetic towards Atlantis, and Pierre Termier is no exception. Termier included a vast amount of evidence for the reality of the sunken continent in a paper entitled 'Atlantis' which he read to the assembled members of the Institut Océanographique of Paris on 30 November, 1912.[5] A general account of Termier's paper also appeared in the *Annual Report of the Smithsonian Institute for 1915*.

Here is a summary. Termier first pictures the Atlantic emptied of its waters. According to the evidence of soundings, he tells us we should, looking at it from above, see two great depressions or valleys, extending north and south parallel with the shores of the Old and New Worlds. The western valley, extending the length of the American coast, is the larger and deeper of the two, and descends more than 6,000 metres below the present sea-level. The eastern sea-level, along the European–African coast line, while apparently narrower and shallower, is more hilly, with numerous submerged peaks resembling those of the Canary and Madeira Islands. Separating these two longitudinal depressions is a central elevated zone known as the mid-Atlantic ridge. It is roughly S-shaped, conforming to the general shape of the Atlantic basin. It begins at Greenland and ends at the 70th parallel South Latitude. The Azores evidently lie on the line of the mid-Atlantic ridge, the nine islands of which forming the group cover a total area or length of about 500 miles; their aggregate area is prolonged very far beneath the waves.

Termier then stresses the fact that the eastern region of the Atlantic bed is in a great volcanic zone. In the Euro-African depression submarine volcanoes are abundant. Most of the islands in this region are composed largely of lava. The same phenomenon occurs in the western or American depression. This would seem to indicate that in the bottom of the Atlantic basin there is a certain mobility of the crust. It is, indeed, still in movement in the extreme eastern zone for a space of about 1,875 miles in breadth, which comprises Iceland, the Azores, Madeira, the Canaries and the Cape Verde Islands. It is the most unstable zone on the Earth's surface, where at any moment unrecorded submarine cataclysms may be taking place.

Termier believed that the land masses in the Atlantic Ocean were submerged in a series of cataclysms spread over thousands of years leaving a few islands still above water. (I gave the same view in my book *Men Among Mankind* published in 1962 – Author.)

He stated:

Geologically speaking Plato's theory of Atlantis is highly probable ... It is entirely reasonable to believe that long after the opening of the Strait of Gibraltar certain of these emerged lands still existed, and among them a marvellous island, separated from the African continent by a chain of other smaller islands. One thing alone remains to be proved –

that the cataclysm which caused this island to disappear was subsequent to the appearance of man in Western Europe. The cataclysm is undoubted. Did men then live who could withstand the reaction and transmit the memory of it? That is the whole question. I do not believe it at all insoluble, though it seems to me that neither geology nor zoology will solve it. These two sciences appear to have told all they can tell, and it is from anthropology, from ethnography, and lastly from oceanography that I am now awaiting the final answer.[6]

Since Termier read his important paper, the science of radiocarbon dating of organic remains, and the progress of oceanographic research, have amply confirmed his beliefs and expectations, and in recent years shown irrefutably that large-scale topographical alterations have occurred in many areas of the Atlantic basin within exceedingly recent geological times. Man *must* have witnessed the convulsion of Nature.

After reviewing the statements and evidence amassed on the Atlantis question, Spence, in another of his books, *The History of Atlantis*, wrote:

From such evidence we may be justified in concluding that the hypothesis of a formerly existing land mass in the Atlantic is by no means based on mere surmise. The fact that geologists of distinction have risked their reputations by testifying in no uncertain manner to the reality of a former Atlantean continent should surely give pause to those who impatiently refuse even to examine the probabilities of the argument so ably upheld. But the most significant consideration which emerges is that this modern expert evidence is almost entirely in favour of the existence of a comparatively recent land mass or masses in the Atlantic, and if we take into consideration the whole of the evidence, and the nature of its sources, it does not seem beyond the bounds of human credence that at a period no earlier than that mentioned by Plato in his *Critias*, viz, 9600 B.C., this ancient continent was still in partial existence, but in process of disintegration – that an island of considerable size, the remnant, perhaps, of the African 'shelf', still lay opposite the entrance to the Mediterranean, and that lesser islands connected it with Europe, Africa, and, perhaps, with our shores.[7]

Soundings taken in the Atlantic by various Admiralty authorities have revealed the existence of a great bank, or elevated region, commencing near the coast of Ireland, traversed by the 53rd parallel, and extending in a southerly direction, embracing the Azores, to the neighbourhood of French Guiana and the estuary of the Amazon and Para rivers. This is the mid-Atlantic ridge, the average depth of which below sea-level is about 9,000 feet, and the same above the floor of the Atlantic. These figures have been obtained by various oceanographic expeditions, such as those of the *Hydra, Porcupine* and *Challenger*, the U.S. ships *Dolphin* and *Gettysburg*, and the German ships *Meteor* and *Gazelle*.

The evidence of the flora and fauna on the islands strewn along this largely submerged ridge, such as the Azores, is complementary to that derived from deep-sea soundings and suboceanic geology, and some of this is worthy of special mention here.

Professor R. F. Scharff, in a paper entitled 'Some Remarks on the Atlantis Problem', read to the Royal Irish Academy, clearly showed that the larger mammalia of the Atlantic islands were not imported thither in historical times. The same authority added that his attempts to trace the history of their origins on the islands '. . . point rather to some of them, at any rate, having reached the latter in the normal way, which is by a land connection with Europe'.[8]

Spence, in *The History of Atlantis*, mentions Professor Simroth, who, writing about the similarity between the slugs of Spain, Portugal, North Africa and the Canaries, concluded that there was probably a broad land connection between these four regions, and that it must have persisted until comparatively recent times.[9]

In his *Testacea Atlantica*, T. V. Wollaston drew attention to the fact that the Mediterranean element in the molluscan fauna of the Atlantic Isles was more noticeable in the Canaries than in the other groups of islands, and boldly stated that the Canaries are the last remnants of a land once more or less continuous with Africa, which had been colonized by molluscs over tracts now submerged.[10]

In this chapter an impressive list of authorities have been quoted, all voicing their considered view that a land mass or masses must have existed in the Atlantic up until quite recently.

In his excellent book, *The Shadow of Atlantis*, Colonel Braghine mentions the research of a German scientist, Major K. Bilau, who 'basing himself on the newest maps and the exact data of the Geographical Institute of Berlin, drew a magnificent map of the bottom of the Atlantic in the region of the Azores'.

As a result of this map and the data contained in it, the German scientist established the truth of Plato's account as follows, quoting from Braghine's book:

Deep under the ocean's waters Atlantis is now reposing and only its highest summits are still visible in the shape of the Azores. Its cold and hot springs, described by the ancient authors, are still flowing there as they flowed many millennia ago. The mountain-lakes of Atlantis have been transformed now into submerged ones. If we follow exactly Plato's indication and seek the site of Poseidonis among the half-submerged summits of the Azores, we will find it to the south of the island of Dollabarata. There, upon an eminence, in the middle of a large and comparatively straight valley, which was well protected from the winds, stood the capital, the magnificent Poseidonis. But we cannot see that mighty centre of an unknown prehistoric culture: between us and the City of the Golden Gate is a layer of water two miles deep. It is strange that the scientists have sought Atlantis everywhere, but have given the least attention to this spot which, after all, was clearly indicated by Plato.[11]

2: The Far Flung Empire

It is a fact that all known accounts of Atlantis, whether Plato's famous narrative or the many traditional and mythological variants, make it the site of an ancient and powerful civilization.

Several writers mention that Atlantis was divided into ten great kingdoms, so it would be reasonable to suppose than more than one marvellous city lies beneath the ocean waves. In the last chapter we referred to the researches and the map compiled by Major K. Bilau. However, Egerton Sykes has furnished me with some data on the sighting of a city beneath the waves of the Atlantic during the war.[1]

Towards the end of 1942, when the pressure on the allies was at its greatest, aircraft of American origin were ferried over the Atlantic from Natal in Brazil to Dakar in French West Africa, adjacent to the site of the historical city of Cerne.

The journey from Dakar to Egypt was performed by easy stages and most of the pilots managed to get a few days' leave in Cairo before returning. One evening in the Turf Club in Cairo, a pilot was overheard chatting to a friend at the bar about a strange sight he had seen on the flight over.

On being approached by Egerton Sykes he explained that in mid-Atlantic, over the Atlantic Ridge, he saw the remains of a city on the Western slope of a submarine mountain. He explained that this was only possible because at the time of his flight the rays of the sun were striking the water at an angle such that they penetrated diagonally to a considerable distance, something which would only occur once in a thousand flights or more.

Unfortunately, the pilot returned to pick up another craft the following day and it was not possible to contact him again. He may possibly still be alive, but one fears not as no further report has ever been received.

Another and completely different city was sighted underwater near the Cape Verde Islands by Captain Andersen of Copenhagen in 1929. The site was off Boavista Island, where a market place was found by a Danish diver. The incident was reported in *Atlantis* for April, 1949.

In support of Bilau's claim, Captain R. Dahl reported finding traces of a sunken area near the surface off Fayal in 1949. This was reported in June of that year in *Atlantis*.

Egerton Sykes ended his special report in these words:

There are Atlantean remains all around the Atlantic, as also on the flanks of the great Atlantic Ridge. As we progress with oceanography there is no doubt but that some of them will be photographed from submarines or other underwater craft. All the evidence needed is available, only we must search for it with care.

More recently, what appears to be the remains of another Atlantean city have been discovered on the other side of the Atlantic Ocean, off the coast of the Bahamas, near Bimini. *The Times*, on Wednesday, 30 June, 1971, carried a report from their science correspondent about the evidence that has been gathered at the site by M. Dimitri Rebikoff, the French underwater explorer. Huge stone blocks about 15 feet to 20 feet square looked as if they had been assembled together by man to form a harbour. It is also known that there are pillars going down for an unknown depth into the muck on the sea-bed, and that these support the stone blocks at their corners. More evidence that it is a man-built edifice.

In his very interesting book, *The Riddle of the Earth*, Comyns Beaumont, writing under the name of Appian Way, remarked:

... To many the most important point in Plato's account of Atlantis is that it was the mother both of Egyptian and Athenian civilization: 'For there was a time, Solon,' said the priest of Sais, in Egypt, 'when the city which is now Athens was first in war, and was pre-eminent for the excellence of her laws and is said to have performed the noblest deeds, and to have had the fairest constitution of any of which tradition tells under the face of heaven. Minerva founded your city a thousand years before ours...'

Beaumont went on to quote from Plato as follows,

'...afterwards there occurred violent earthquakes and floods, and in a single day and night of rain all your warlike men in a body sunk into the earth, and the island of Atlantis in like manner disappeared and was sunk beneath the sea.'[2]

Atlantis was alluded to in one way or another by several other ancient authors, such as Theopompus (circa 378–300 B.C.), who was noted for his accuracy. Aelian, in the third volume of his *Varia Hist.*, says that Theopompus, who lived at Chios, stated that Atlantis was inhabited by men of 'gigantic size', who were very long-lived, and that gold was more abundant than iron.[3]

The influence of Atlantean civilization on ancient Egypt, the Babylonians, the Phoenicians, the Greeks, the Romans, and even on the Scandinavians, on the east side of the Atlantic, is quite remarkable. The same influence penetrated in the other direction into what are now parts of the United States, as well as Central America, and into large parts of South America, especially in Bolivia, Brazil, Colombia and Peru. The Atlantean Empire covered a great portion of the earth.

Donnelly, in *Atlantis: The Antediluvian World*, points out that the ancient religion in Atlantis was sun worship.

The Egyptians worshipped the sun under the name of Ra; the Hindoos worshipped the sun under the name of Rama; while the great festival of the Sun, of the Peruvians, was called Raymi.[4]

He goes on to state that the gods of the Greeks on Mt. Olympus were really Atlantean kings, and much the same goes for the gods of the Romans and Phoenicians.

The Greeks, too young to have shared in the religion of Atlantis, but preserving some memory of that great country and its history, proceeded to convert its kings into gods, and to depict Atlantis itself as the heaven of the human race. Thus we find a great solar or nature worship in the elder nations, while Greece has nothing but an incongruous jumble of gods and goddesses, who are born and eat and drink and make love and ravish and steal and die; and who are worshipped as immortal in presence of the very monuments that testify to their death.[5]

Later on, Donnelly, quoting from Murray's *Mythology*, wrote:

Another proof that the gods of the Greeks were but the deified kings of Atlantis is found in the fact that 'the gods were not looked upon as having created the world'. They succeeded to the management of a world already in existence.[6]

After discussing the way of life on Atlantis, Donnelly continued:

This blessed land answers to the description of Atlantis. It was an island full of wonders. It lay spread out in the ocean 'like a disc, with the mountains rising from it' (Murray's *Mythology*). On the highest point of this mountain dwelt Zeus (the king), 'while the mansions of the other deities were arranged upon plateaux, or in ravines lower down the mountain. These deities, including Zeus, were twelve in number: Zeus (or Jupiter), Hera (or Juno), Poseidon (or Neptune), Demeter (or Ceres), Apollo, Artemis (or Diana), Hephaestos (or Vulcan), Pallas Athena (or Minerva), Ares (or Mars), Aphrodite (or Venus), Hermes (or Mercury), and Hestia (or Vesta).' These were doubtless the twelve gods from whom the Egyptians derived their kings. Where two names are given to a deity in the above list, the first name is that bestowed by the Greeks, the last that given by the Romans.[7]

Incidentally, you will notice that Apollo is a god in both the Greek and Roman pantheons.

Although there is a Mt. Olympus in Greece, Donnelly states that 'Greek tradition located the island in which Olympus was situated "in the far west", "in the ocean beyond Africa", "on the western boundary of the known world", "where the sun shone when it had ceased to shine on Greece", and where the mighty Atlas "held up the heavens". And Plato tells us that the land where Poseidon and Atlas rules was Atlantis.'

Far away to the west across what is now the Atlantic Ocean lies the New World. It is a strange fact that the sign of the swastika, one of the oldest symbols in the world, which Hitler debased by reversing and adopting as a symbol for his Nazi party, is found on both sides of the Atlantic Ocean.

Braghine wrote:

We are surprised also by the resemblance between some American sacred symbols and the corresponding symbols of the ancient Europeans. We see, for instance, the sign of the swastika not only on the most ancient Aryan monuments; but also on the prehistoric American ones; the head of the Gorgon, the symbol of divine knowledge, we can meet with not only on the classical monuments, but also in Mexican ruins and on the inscrutable Stone of Chavin, a magnificent relic of the Tiahuanaco culture ...

And later on:

Professor Leo Frobenius has established some resemblances between the mysterious Etruscans and certain Indian tribes. It seems likely that a great deal of ancient European folklore was borrowed by the prehistoric Europeans from certain ancient American races, the Atlanteans in this case serving as a bridge between the Europeans and Americans....[8]

It is of interest to note that Pastor Jurgen Spanuth has recently suggested that Atlantis lay in the North Sea on the island of Heligoland. This theory was partly based on the premise that the old name for Heligoland was Atland.

Peter Kolosimo, in his book *Timeless Earth*, wrote:

On the other hand, there are Amerindian legends of an 'Aztland' which was involved in a catastrophe much earlier than that of the Medinet Habu inscriptions; and the proponents of a Nordic Atlantis have difficulty in explaining the references by Plato and Theopompus to a land beyond the Pillars of Hercules.[9]

However, as Kolosimo adds:

Our verdict on Spanuth's theory must therefore be that, while we cannot accept that Heligoland and Atlantis are identical, it is quite possible that the last Atlanteans of northern Europe had their headquarters in the region he describes.[10]

Brazil has great connections with Atlantis. H. T. Wilkins in *Mysteries of Ancient South America* wrote: 'Hy or Royal Brazil is the name given in the old Irish Legends to a lost golden world ...'[11]

The Atlanteans of old were well versed in occult matters and knew that a catastrophe of overwhelming consequences was imminent and sent forth bearded, white men from their western Empire of Hy-Brazil to civilize the savage indians of Central America, and Colombia, Peru and Bolivia, in South America. In the first chapter a brief reference was made to these bearded white men.

Braghine tells us:

The legends of the American races and tribes concerning great reformers, leaders and missionaries who from time to time appeared among the natives also sustain our hypothesis of the cultural mission of the Atlanteans in the prehistoric world. There were it seems eight such reformers: in Peru, Manco Capac, Viracocha, and Pachacamac; in Colombia, Bochica, among the Tupis, Tupan; in Yucatan, It-Zamna, or Zamna; in Mexico, Quetzal-Coatl (called in Guatemala 'Gucamatz', and in Yucatan, 'Cuculcna'); and in Brazil and Paraguay, Zume (called by the Caribs 'Tamu', by the Arovacs 'Camu' and by the Carayas 'Caboy'). The Peruvian myth concerning Viracocha resembles the Colombian myth concerning Bochica.

All these men, or gods, were sages, all came from some unknown land to the east of America, all wore long beards, all were white-skinned and their end was everywhere the same: their mission fulfilled, the sages mysteriously disappeared, promising to return to their beloved people later on. In all these Central and South American legends are hidden, it seems, the same facts: from time to time Atlantean missionaries appeared in America and their activity was clothed later on by poetry and religion. I can mention in favour of this hypothesis the following fact: one of the above named reformers, Quetzal-Coatl, introduced into Mexico the cult of Tlaloc, or the Mexican Poseidon, who was the god of the sea, water and rains. We know that the cult of Poseidon was the most important in Atlantis, or Poseidonis.[12]

All this once again indicates the tremendous influence and impact of the Atlantean culture in prehistoric times. In its heyday, Atlantis must have been an empire of such an extent and power as this world has never known since.

3 :   A Discovery greater than Troy

In 1929, a map was discovered in the Sultan's palace in Constantinople, signed by a Turkish admiral, one Piri Ibn Haji Memmed. It was dated 1513 and it is known as the Piri Re'is map. The word Re'is means admiral.

The whole tremendous story of this fascinating map is to be found in Professor Charles H. Hapgood's book, *Maps of the Ancient Sea Kings – Evidence of Advanced Civilization in the Ice Age!*

Hapgood wrote :

No more was heard of it until, by a series of curious chances, it aroused attention in Washington, D.C., in 1956. A Turkish naval officer had brought a copy of the map to the U.S. Navy Hydrographic Office as a gift (although, unknown to him, facsimiles already existed in the Library of Congress and other leading libraries in the United States). The map had been referred to a cartographer on the staff, M. I. Walters.[1]

Subsequently, Walters passed the map to a friend, Captain Arlington H. Mallery, who had much experience in studying old maps.

There were, at first, three points of interest : (1) this map differed from all other maps of America drawn in the 16th century, in that it showed South America and Africa in correct relative longitudes, (2) Piri Re'is stated that part of the map had been based on one drawn by Columbus, and (3) Mallery considered that part of the map showed places on the coast of Queen Maud Land in Antarctica now hidden under the ice cap. This last point implied that the coast had been mapped before the ice appeared!

In any case, this was considered truly fantastic as the Antarctic continent was only discovered in the early 19th century.

Other scientists and cartographers were called in by Mallery, including the Reverend Daniel L. Lineham, director of the Weston Observatory of Boston College, and the Reverend Francis Heyden, Director of the Georgetown University Observatory.

The Reverend Lineham and Mr. Walters joined Mallery in a radio panel discussion sponsored by Georgetown University.

Subsequently, Professor Charles H. Hapgood started a study course with his students at Keene State College of the University of New Hampshire, to investigate the Piri Re'is map. The story of their work and the conclusions arrived at from their study can be found in his wonderful book. Other old maps known to scholars, such as the so-called Portolano charts of the Middle Ages, and others, were brought into the research work.

The results of the work undertaken by Hapgood and his team indicate that the originals from which the Piri Re'is map (dated A.D. 1513) was compiled must have been made before the last ice age. In order to undertake such a task all that long time ago, the cartographers of that era must have photographed the places on the map from the air. The conclusion must be that some amazing civilization had flying machines and cameras over 10,000 years ago!

I am not advancing this important discovery in support of a physical Atlantis, as no land mass or masses, now under the waters, appear on the Piri Re'is map, but it is evidence that a very advanced civilization was around in times before recorded history began, and it is possible that the information for the preparation of the originals that Piri Re'is worked from in the marking of his own map, was handed down by the survivors of the sinking of Poseidonis.

Earlier in this book it was suggested that Atlantis went under the Atlantic Ocean in a series of three catastrophes spread over millennia. According to Plato, the last island of Atlantis, namely Poseidonis, was submerged about 9500 B.C. — well over 11,500 years ago. However, it is now the consensus of scientific opinion that the last ice age started about 10,000 years ago; in other words, some 1,500 years after Poseidonis sank beneath the waves. Some parts of the world may not have been so devastatingly affected by this last catastrophe, though I have indicated in this book that it was pretty widespread. It seems a possibility that some survivors from the Atlantean civilization or their descendants provided the material for the originals from which Piri Re'is made his map.

In any case, whatever further research discloses, Mallery's discovery of the Piri Re'is map and its potential significance, together with Hapgood's work confirming the implications behind it all, will one day be realized to be of even greater importance than Schliemann's discovery of Troy.

4: Enigma of Tiahuanaco

In this chapter I propose to devote special attention to what may well be the oldest collection of ruined edifices in the New World. Ancient writers have referred to the Atlanteans as being of gigantic size, and it is important to realize that they built on a titanic or cyclopean scale. In a later chapter we will be discussing the gigantic tunnel systems built by these amazing people.

The ruins at Tiahuanaco are an example of this building in a king-size style. First, it should be stated that Tiahuanaco is situated on the Andean Altiplano at an elevation in excess of 12,500 feet above sea-level, close by Lake Titicaca, and not far from the border of Bolivia and Peru.

Dealing with the problem of this amazing elevation, Sir Clemens Markham, in *The Incas of Peru*, wrote:

There is a mystery still unsolved on the plateau of Lake Titicaca, which, if stone could speak, would reveal a story of deepest interest. Much of the difficulty in the solution of this mystery is caused by the nature of the region, in the present day, where the enigma still defies explanation.[1]

Then two pages on, he added:

Such a region is only capable of sustaining a scanty population of hardy mountaineers and labourers. The mystery consists in the existence of a great city at the southern side of the lake...[2]

Elaborating upon a suggestion advanced by Sir Leonard Darwin, the then president of the Royal Geographical Society in London, that the Titicaca basin had risen appreciably after the erection of the original edifices at Tiahuanaco, Sir Clemens remarked:

Is such an idea beyond the bounds of possibility? ... maize would then ripen in the basin of Lake Titicaca, and the site of the ruins of Tiahuanaco would support the necessary population ...[3]

A fact to remember when arguing along these lines is that the whole character of the local country and the extent of Lake Titicaca would have been different, with a consequent difference in climatic conditions. The foremost authority on the Tiahuanacan ruins and cultures, Professor Arthur Posnansky, in his book, *Tiahuanaco: The Cradle of American Man*, has said of this problem:

At the present time, the plateau of the Andes is inhospitable and almost sterile. With the present climate, it would not have been suitable in any period as the asylum for great human masses ... Today this region is at a very great heignt above sea-level. In remote times it was lower.[4]

At this point in the argument, I would like to quote from my book, *Men Among Mankind*; referring to a major catastrophe affecting Atlantis some 15,000 years ago, I postulated in that book, as has been re-affirmed in this one, that the lost continent went down in three stages.

... These events, coupled with climatic changes, altered the face of the globe. The continuous wrenching, twisting and turning of the earth in this gargantuan cosmic upheaval with Luna, caused faults to form on the face of the world and mountains to arise on its surface. The Rocky Mountains, the Cascade Range and the Andes, in the Americas, together with the Himalayas in Asia and the Alps in Europe, were either not there previously or had not achieved anything like their present range and height. Immanuel Velikovsky wrote that 'The great massif of the Himalayas rose to its present height in the age of modern, actually historical man'.[5,6]

Colonel P. H. Fawcett, who mysteriously disappeared in the Brazilian Matto Grosso during 1925, travelled all over Peru and Bolivia in the first two decades of this century, and came to much the same conclusions about the age of

Tiahuanaco. He believed it to have been destroyed by terrible seismic upheavals accompanying the elevation of the Andes to their present height.[7]

Harold T. Wilkins, in *Mysteries of Ancient South America*, concluded that Tiahuanaco was of great antiquity, and in the following passage associated the ruins with giants.

One may be forgiven, when contemplating the amazing command of these ancient engineers and masons over vast masses of rock in a way that can hardly be rivalled by modern engineers with all their wonderful techniques and power appliances, for speculating whether they were a race of giants in stature?[8]

H. S. Bellamy, in *Built Before the Flood: The Problem of the Tiahuanaco Ruins*, remarked:

The measurements of some of the buildings of Tiahuanaco are astounding. The 'fortress' of Akapana measures about 650 feet by 100 feet (roughly equal to the area of the Tower of London, inside the Moat); the outer walls of the Great Sun Temple of Kalacasaye measure about 440 by 390 feet (roughly equal to the area of Trafalgar Square); those of the 'Palace of the Black-White-and-Red Stairs', also called the 'Palace of the Sarcophagi', measure 220 by 180 feet (roughly equal to the area of Leicester Square). All the great buildings of Tiahuanaco, except small parts of them, were open to the sky, and evidently gathering places for vast multitudes who met for political, religious and social purposes...[9]

One reason for considering that Tiahuanaco was built by a race of giants is the fact that there were enormous foundation slabs, and in the structures themselves huge blocks were used. No small elements or bricks were involved in the building of Tiahuanaco.

Bellamy considered that this type of architecture was dictated by the exigencies of nature. No mortar was used. The walls were built in such a way as to be extremely solid but also elastic, which would render them to some extent earthquake-proof.[10]

Incidentally, the walls of some of the Tiahuanaco-like ruins of Siminake are as much as ten feet thick, another factor consistent with the earthquake menace which dictated this way of building.

A. H. Verrill and R. Verrill, both of whom visited and surveyed Tiahuanaco, state that the largest worked block there measures 36 feet by 7 feet and must weigh between 175 and 200 tons.[11]

Nearly every stone at Tiahuanaco is expertly and micro-accurately cut and polished, nicked, mortized and, occasionally, even bevelled. So astonishing is it that Squier, in *Peru, Incidents of Travel and Exploration in the Land of the Incas*, wrote:

In no part of the world have I seen stones cut with such mathematical precision and admirable skill as in Peru; and in no part of Peru are there any to surpass those which are scattered over the plains of Tiahuanaco.[12]

Earlier in this chapter I quoted from one of my earlier books implying that Tiahuanaco was raised to its present position in a catastrophe 15,000 years ago. In that work, I also described the Gate of the Sun at Tiahuanaco on which is carved a figure of the Sun, surrounded by winged messengers. There is also sculptured on the gateway a very precise astronomical calendar.

Alexandre Kazantsev, the well-known Russian scientist, visited Tiahuanaco a few years ago. Incidentally, he discovered, like so many others that have visited the area, that the water in Lake Titicaca is saline and that there are sea shells on the beach, and traces of an old harbour. All this surely indicates that millennia ago, before the catastrophe that overtook the world, Lake Titicaca and Tiahuanaco were at sea-level, and that the lake was probably a bay or inlet by the sea.

However, I am digressing from the astronomical calendar on the Gate of the Sun, though it was an important digression, I think you will agree.

Kazantsev estimated the Gate of the Sun to have been built between 12,000 and 15,000 years ago. He said that for 15,000 years our Earth has turned on its axis at almost the same rate. Then, if that is the case, he asked, why should this calendar on the Gate of the Sun at Tiahuanaco be so different from our known ones?

You see, Kazantsev discovered that the Tiahuanaco calendar shows a year of 290 days (not 365), composed of twelve months (ten of 24 days, that is 240; and two of 25, that is 50. Total 290). The Russian scientist stated that Professor Girov and others have agreed that the calendar on the Gate of the Sun is the oldest in the world. The implications of this are tremendous!

If our calendar has remained more or less the same for 15,000 years, and the calendar at Tiahuanaco describes a completely different one of 290 days, which I am told is similar to the Venusian length of a year, then this surely proves that this particular catastrophe happened around 15,000 years ago, as I have been advocating.[13]

Tiahuanaco today stands high up in the Andes, a lonely memorial to the mysterious race who built those amazing edifices. There is some evidence that the monoliths were not entirely finished when the catastrophe struck and caused a whole city and a lake to be raised to a height of 12,500 feet above sea-level. Forgive me for repeating this, but the whole thought, as I am sure you will appreciate, is absolutely staggering!

There seems to be a very likely connection between the race of Atlantean giants who built mysterious Tiahuanaco and those who erected the 550 colossal stone figures of men looking disdainfully inland on the tall cliffs of Easter Island, far away in the Pacific Ocean.

Thor Heyerdahl, as the result of his epic voyage from South America to the South Seas on his raft, the *Kon-Tiki*, evidently came to that conclusion. He considered that the race of people who built Tiahuanaco were the same race who constructed the fantastic figures on Easter Island, and that they got to the South Seas in the same way that he did.[14] I am not sure whether he is correct on the last score, as there is good reason to think that the Atlanteans had flying machines. After all, we have pointed out in the last chapter when discussing the fabulous Piri Re'is Map that those cartographers who compiled the originals from which the map was prepared must have had flying machines to do the work. True, this might have been done three or four thousand years later, but a race of people who were capable of building such wonderful buildings at Tiahuanaco, Easter Island and the platform at Baalbeck in the Lebanon, and the fantastic tunnel systems we will be describing later, could well have had flying machines. Indeed, all the legends indicate that they came from outer space! So, I doubt if they would have sailed from South America in some kind of raft like Heyerdahl did. This in no way is intended to take any credit away from that splendid man for his great epic voyage and fine seamanship. He certainly proved that they could have done the journey like him that way, but somehow I don't think the Atlanteans used rafts. They flew through the air with the greatest of ease.

Incidentally, the stone edifices on Easter Island were unfinished too, indicating that the builders there were involved in the catastrophe that engulfed the world at that time.

There is yet another 'out of this world' structure on our planet today, which also goes to illustrate the extraordinary capabilities the ancients possessed in the art of building.

I refer to the ruins of Baalbeck, which lie at a height of 3,500 feet, to the north east of Beirut in the Lebanon.

In *Men Among Mankind* I wrote:

The Romans built magnificent temples to their gods upon, in the words of Mark Twain, 'massive sub-structures that might support a world almost. The material used is blocks of stone as large as an omnibus...'

I later continued as follows:

The massive sub-structures referred to by Mark Twain, which form the huge platform on which the Great Temple is built, are truly amazing. He wrote that one stretch of the platform, composed of only three stones, was nearly 200 feet in length! They are thirteen feet square, two of them being sixty-four feet and the third sixty-nine feet long, and built into the massive wall twenty feet above the ground.

It can easily be gathered from the aforementioned data that the stones used at Baalbeck were far bigger than anything at Tiahuanaco. In that earlier book from which I have just quoted, I went on to write,

No one, so far, has come up with the answer as to who built the massive platform at Baalbeck, upon which the Romans are known to have constructed a very long time afterwards their wonderful temples.[15]

Apparently, the platform at Baalbeck was not entirely completed either. I wrote:

The quarry from which these colossal stones at Baalbeck were taken is a quarter of a mile away from the platform and at a much lower level. Mark Twain relates how in a pit lay a similar stone, 'the mate of the largest stone in the ruins'. What is more, it lies there, 'squared and ready for the builder's hands, a solid mass fourteen feet by seventeen feet wide and seventy feet long'.

What caused that tremendous block of masonry intended for the great solid block at Baalbeck to be abandoned leaving the work unfinished?[16]

In this chapter it has been shown that in antediluvian times there was a great civilization that built tremendous edifices all over the world, and the remains of three of these survive today, as constant reminders of a former great culture that existed on this planet. Tiahuanaco, high up in the Andes, Easter Island in the South Seas, and finally, at Baalbeck in the Lebanon. In previous books I have discussed the Great Pyramid in Egypt, Stonehenge and the remarkable serpentine figures at Avebury, similar constructions at Carnac in France, and we could mention the Fortress of Cuzco, built with 200-ton stones. The dates of all these last mentioned edifices are very controversial, though I consider them all to have a much greater antiquity than is credited to them by orthodox scientists. However, the three we have dealt with in this chapter belong to a great era some millennia ago, and are all irrevocably connected with a great catastrophe that took place some 15,000 years ago, and changed the shape of the world. Very much more than did the final catastrophe in 9500 B.C. related by Plato, which saw the last island of Atlantis – that of Poseidonis, sink beneath the ocean.

There is increasing evidence that many millennia ago there came to this earth from outer space a race of people who were able to design and build temples, palaces and other edifices, in a way that nobody can do today, despite all our modern techniques. They were craftsmen of a very unusual order, descended from the gods. They were the Atlanteans who civilized the world of their time.

It was truly an incredible age.

5: Giants and Titans

The Bible tells us that there was a war in heaven.

And there was war in heaven: Michael and his angels fought against the dragon; and the dragon fought and his angels.

And prevailed not; neither was their place found any more in heaven.

And the great dragon was cast out, that old serpent, called the Devil, and Satan, which deceiveth the whole world; he was cast out into the earth, and his angels were cast out with him.

The Book of Revelation. XIII, 7–9

It would seem that this was a war on a cosmic scale that must have been a pretty big affair, making our two recent world wars comparatively insignificant, quite puny in fact. That is, if you take the biblical account literally.

We do know from another biblical story that the 'fallen angels' or 'sons of God' did arrive on Earth and were soon busy fraternizing and copulating with the daughters of men. (Genesis 6: 1–2, 4.)

It would seem that the 'sons of God', fallen though they may have been, were still capable of using what to the very primitive inhabitants of Earth must have seemed like supernatural powers.

We have already mentioned earlier that these were the original gods of the ancient Egyptians, the Phoenicians, the Romans and the Greeks.

The war that had started in heaven continued for long afterwards on earth between the various gods. I think that they were invaded from outer space after they arrived here, and this view is held by Erich von Daniken. We will be discussing this theory in a later chapter. Anyway, conflict went on in a very big way and for a long time there was constant battle between various gods. As a result of their interbreeding with those beings who were already on Earth, they spawned terrible monsters and the result was diabolical. They also tried to create new forms of life in the underground caverns of the world and what happened is related in Greek mythology.

H. A. Guerber, in his book *The Myths of Greece and Rome*, referring to the children of Gaea and Uranus, wrote:

... They had not dwelt long on the summit of Mount Olympus before they found themselves the parents of twelve gigantic children, whose strength was such that their father, Uranus, greatly feared them. To prevent their ever making use of it against him he seized them immediately after their birth, hurled them down into a dark abyss called Tartarus, and there chained them fast. These giants were called 'Titans', and we still use the word 'Titanic' to describe something of vast size. Thus early did the giant appear in legend.

This chasm was situated far under the earth; and Uranus knew that his sons (Oceanus, Coeus, Creus, Hyperion, Iapetus and Cronus), as well as his six daughters, the Titanides (Ilia, Rhea, Themis, Thetis, Mnemosyne and Phoebe), could not easily escape from its cavernous depths...[1]

There are constant references throughout Greek mythology to Tartarus or Hades, a place far down under the earth, the prison house of the Lower World. It is part of our argument that Atlantis existed and that the gods of Greek mythology were originally the kings of Atlantis, later dividing the ten kingdoms that made up the whole Empire between them, under the overall rule of Zeus. The Atlantic area was given to Poseidon (after whom the island of Poseidonis was named), and the underworld to Pluto. If all these surface kingdoms of Atlantis were considered real by the ancient writers, then why should not the Lower World of Tartarus be equally real?

I consider the hollow Earth to be a fact, and in the second part of this book will set before you up-to-date proof. At this stage we can well study the frequent mention of Tartarus in the legends. It is appreciated that mythology is not a collection of facts but of myths. However, behind all these stories there may well lie something close to truth – something so devastating that all our conceptions of the geography of the Earth will have to be revised.

It is not necessary to go into Greek mythology too deeply here. Suffice it to state that Cronus escaped from Tartarus with the aid of his mother, Gaea, and overcame his father, Uranus, while asleep. He then set free his brothers and sisters, and became the new king.

His father had cursed him, foretelling that one day he, Cronus, would in turn be supplanted by his own children. The time came when his wife Rhea gave birth to a son. When Rhea offered him the baby to hold, Cronus recollecting his father's curse, swallowed the child while Rhea looked on in horror.

Each time Rhea had a child, it would meet with the same fate. Finally, when Zeus her youngest was born, she decided to trick her husband. She placed a large stone in swaddling clothes and offered it to Cronus who swallowed it.

Meanwhile, Rhea had arranged for Zeus to be looked after by the Melian nymphs who hid him in a cave on Mount Ida.

Subsequently, when Zeus was a grown man he attacked and overcame his father in a terrific struggle. Cronus was given a special potion prepared by Metis, daughter of Oceanus. This caused him to vomit up the children and the stone that he had swallowed.

Zeus gave his brothers and sisters a share of his domain, and some of the Titans, notably Oceanus, Hyperion and Themis, gave their allegiance to the new king. However, the others would not have Zeus as their king, and so began a terrible conflict – the Revolt of the Titans.

The Titans began a furious attack on Mt. Olympus. Zeus, realizing that he was outnumbered, released the

Cyclopes and the Hecatoncheires, who had also been languishing in Tartarus. The Cyclopes agreed to let him have thunderbolts, weapons which they knew how to make! There is something here very reminiscent of twentieth-century warfare. And the Hecatoncheires put their hundred-handed arms at his disposal. I am wondering if this story has not got a little distorted while being passed on to us by the ancient Greeks who did not have the modern weapons that we do, today. The ancients were passing on legends of their gods who lived thousands of years before them. This is pure speculation, but I am wondering if the Hecatoncheires had got the ability to construct something like giant tanks which were armed with one hundred guns or weapons?

The war lasted for ten long years. Zeus, himself, took part hurling thunderbolts incessantly. The Titans were eventually overcome, and some of them were flung into Tartarus once more.

Zeus had scarcely overcome the Titans when he found himself involved in a new war, this time against the Giants.

These Giants had apparently been conceived, according to the story, from the blood of the mutilated Uranus. I shall have some ideas of my own to give you later about this.

These new giants were terrible to behold. They had legs like serpents and their feet consisted of the heads of snakes. They attacked Mt. Olympus in force, tearing up mountains and piling them one on the other. However, the Olympians stood their ground, but it was eventually due to a semi-divine mortal, Hercules, who managed to defeat the giant, Alcyoneus, that the battle was won. It is very important to note that these particular giants were monstrous mutants.

Finally, Gaea, made one more effort on behalf of her Titan children. According to the *Larousse Encyclopaedia of Mythology*, 'Gaea, however, could not resign herself to the defeat of her children. Against Zeus she raised up a final monster, Typhoeus, whom she had borne to Tartarus...'[2]

There is no such person as Tartarus. It is the name of the underworld prison-house, sometimes called Hades. The above quotation is a clear indication that this monster was manufactured in Tartarus!

At first Zeus stood firm against this dreadful monster but he was taken prisoner by Typhoeus and kept captive in Cilicia. After being rescued by Hermes, Zeus finally overcame the monster by using his thunderbolts with great skill. After this, peace came to the world. Zeus was now truly in command. As mentioned earlier he divided up his realm among his brothers, and looked after all these areas as a kind of supreme Emperor.

Did these mythological events take place? Obviously, the myths have got distorted in many ways and mixed up, as a result of all the terrible cataclysms that overcame the earth many millennia ago. However, there is a saying, that 'where there is smoke, there is fire', and in my opinion, there does seem to be an awful lot of smoke!

Obviously, some of the very early myths relating to Uranus and Cronus deal with the creation of the world. However, the subsequent stories, covering the wars of the Giants and Titans, may well have been colossal holocausts that took place in Atlantis. Furthermore, the thunderbolts and suggestions of other advanced weapons add a note of reality to these legends.

I think that after Zeus finally defeated all his enemies the Golden Age of Atlantis set in, and probably lasted for thousands of years. It would be interesting to question here the actual dating of the bearded white men who came from Atlantis to Central and South America, to civilize the natives of those countries and pass on to them some of the Atlantean culture. Did they perform their missions before the catastrophe of 15,000 years ago, which destroyed Tiahuanaco, and caused the work at Easter Island and Baalbeck to be abandoned? I think that they did.

The Atlanteans, by all accounts, prior to the submergence of Poseidonis in 9500 B.C. had gradually got very materialistic and aggressive, leading to their war against the ancient Greeks, described by Diodorus, a Roman writer. While this conflict was taking place the catastrophe ensued, the Greek army was swallowed up into the earth and Poseidonis sank under the waters.

The war between the Atlanteans and the Greeks was no invention on the part of Diodorus, as accounts of it were in circulation centuries before his time.

It should by now be clear that the wars of the Giants and the Titans, and the final one against the ancient Greeks, were all part of the history of Atlantis. Although a great deal of the story of these terrible conflicts is shrouded in the mists of both antiquity and mythology, the basic picture can be discerned, albeit dimly. The result is a long panoramic narrative in the form of legends and myths telling us of gods that came from outer space, who ruled over Atlantis and were the progenitors of our own civilization. They also fought terrible wars, and in the underground world of Tartarus made grotesque monsters and giants with reptilian legs, that turned on the gods themselves.

6: Atlantean Tunnel Systems

The awe-inspiring megalithic buildings around the world erected by the Atlanteans have already been discussed. In writing about Tiahuanaco, stress was laid on the fact that this city was constructed in an unusual manner to make it earthquake-proof.

The world in those far-off days was physically very unstable. For this reason, too, the Atlanteans built fantastic tunnel systems in which refuge could be taken, if necessary, from both the onslaughts of nature and attacks from outer space.

Erich von Daniken in his remarkable book, *The Gold of the Gods*, tells of 'A gigantic system of tunnels, thousands of miles in length' extending underneath Ecuador and Peru. This system of both interlinking caves and tunnels was discovered by Jan Moricz in 1965.[1]

Von Daniken related that a tunnel led into a huge hall where there were stone and metal objects, including statues of many kinds of animals made of solid gold. Furthermore, there was a metal library consisting of metal plaques (leaves) with writing on them in an unknown language, which Moricz thinks may contain a history of humanity and details about a vanished civilization.

Von Daniken stated that the tunnels under Ecuador and Peru have walls that are smooth and 'often seem to be polished'. He realized that these tunnels had not been hacked out with axes, but constructed by much more sophisticated means.

In his book he suggested that the builders of the tunnels used a combination of thermal drills and electron ray guns. In von Daniken's words:

...If the drill came up against some exceptionally hard geological strata, these could be blasted by a few well-aimed shots with the gun. Then the armoured thermal drill would attack the resulting blocks and heat the mass of debris to the liquid state. As soon as the liquid rock cooled down, it would form a diamond-hard glaze. The tunnel system would be safe against infiltration by water, and supports for the chamber would be superfluous.[2]

Towards the end of his book, von Daniken put forward a most interesting theory concerning a specific reason as to why the tunnels were built. This is something quite apart from the dangers of seismic activity which I have already covered, and was a very real threat, too.

He suggested that in remote times a cosmic battle took place among people who looked very much like ourselves. The losers apparently got away in a spaceship. Personally, I would have credited them with more than one spaceship, but that is probably carping a bit unnecessarily.

He then mentions the 'gas masks' the losers wore in what was to them our different atmosphere, and refers to the various helmets and breathing apparatus seen in cave dwellings.

Von Daniken then stated that the victors – those that remained on this planet – 'burrowed deep into the earth and made the tunnel systems out of fear of their pursuers who were equipped with every kind of technical aid.'[3]

Then, to throw their opponents completely off the track, they set up broadcasting stations on the fifth planet of our solar system, then existing between Mars and Jupiter. These stations kept sending out coded reports.

The enemy, von Daniken suggested, fell for this ruse, and destroyed the fifth planet with a terrific explosion. The debris from the exploded planet spread through what is now called 'The Asteroid Belt'. This area consists of thousands of asteroids and small lumps of stones. As von Daniken puts it, '... planets do not "explode" by themselves someone makes them explode!'[4]

I think that this is a most fascinating and plausible concept, and it would seem that the weapons used in those very remote times were even more lethal than in our own day and age. In this connection, I am wondering what those 'thunderbolts' really were, that Zeus and the other gods tossed around.

Peter Kolosimo, in *Timeless Earth*, writes of a tunnel system connecting Lima to Cuzco, and from there continuing to the Bolivian border. He wrote:

Apart from the lure of gain, these tunnels present a fascinating archaeological problem. Scholars agree that they were not made by the Incas themselves, who used them but were ignorant of their origin. They are in fact so imposing that it does not seem absurd to conjecture, as some scientists have done, that they are the handiwork of an unknown race of giants.[5]

Harold T. Wilkins, in his book *Mysteries of Ancient South America*, was probably describing the same tunnel system when he stated:

One of the approaches to the great tunnels lay, and still lies, near old Cuzco, 'but it is masked beyond discovery'. This hidden approach leads directly into an immense 'subterranean', which runs from Cuzco to Lima, *as the crow flies, a distance of 380 miles*! Then, turning southwards, *the great tunnel extends into what, until about 1868, was modern Bolivia, around 900 miles*! ...[6]

Wilkins also referred to some tunnels in the West Indies:

Similar strange tunnels of incredibly ancient date, and unknown origin, in the West Indies, were brought to the attention of Christopher Columbus, when he visited Martinique. No doubt the white, Atlantean race built splendid cities in what are now West Indian islands, but which, at that far-off date may have formed part of a now submerged, middle American continent, whose name is commemorated in the word: 'Antilles'. A curious tradition of the old world of Asia is that old Atlantis had a network of labyrinthine tunnels and passages running in all directions, in the day when the land bridge between the drowned land and Africa on one side, and old Brazil on the other, existed. In Atlantis, the tunnels were used for necromantic and black magic cults...[7]

Kolosimo pointed out that tunnel systems are to be found all over the world. Apart from South America, he listed California, Virginia, Hawaii, Oceania and Asia. In Europe there are tunnels in Sweden and Czechoslovakia; and, in the Mediterranean area, in the Balearics and Malta. He added:

A huge tunnel, some thirty miles of which have been explored, runs between Spain and Morocco, and many believe that this is how the 'Barbary Apes', which are otherwise unknown in Europe, reached Gibraltar.[8]

Indeed, Kolosimo wrote:

It has even been suggested that these Cyclopean galleries form a network connecting the most distant parts of our planet.[9]

Easter Island has already been mentioned in regard to the enigmatic figures on the cliffs, but who constructed the tunnels that lead out under the sea, and for what purpose?

Wilkins has more to tell us about the ancient tunnel systems:

Among the Mongolian tribes of Inner Mongolia, even today, there are traditions about tunnels and subterranean worlds which sound as fantastic as anything in modern novels. One legend – if it be that! – says that the tunnels lead to a subterranean world of antediluvian descent somewhere in a recess of Afghanistan, or in the region of the Hindu Kush...

It is even given a name – Agharti. The legend adds that a labyrinth of tunnels and underground passages is extended in a series of links connecting Agharti with all other such subterranean worlds! ... The subterranean world, it is said, is lit by a strange green luminescence which favours the growth of crops and is conducive to length of days and health.[10]

This last account is of special interest as Kolosimo refers to this green fluorescence in another part of the world. He writes in *Timeless Earth* about a strange 'bottomless well' in Azerbaijan in the Soviet Union. Apparently, a bluish light comes from its wall and odd noises are heard. Eventually, after investigating and exploring, scientists found a whole system of tunnels connecting with other ones in Georgia and all over the Caucasus.[11]

After describing these tunnels, which are regular in form, and, he stated, almost identical with similar ones in Central America, Kolosimo went on to tell us that they are part of a huge system even connecting with Iran and, moreover, with the tunnels of China, Tibet and Mongolia.[12]

Now, referring back to Wilkins' account of a subterranean world called Agharti, which was said to be lit by a strange green luminescence, Kolosimo has this to say:

The Tibetans believe that the tunnels are citadels, the last of which still afford refuge to the survivors of an immense cataclysm. This unknown people is said to make use of an underground source of energy which replaces that of the sun, causing plants to breed and prolonging human life. It is supposed to give out a green fluorescence, and it is curious that we also meet with this idea in American legend...[13]

In the latter part of this book we will be relating the strange story of the Green Children of Wolfpittes, which may have a special bearing on what has just been told.

Anyway, enough has been written here to indicate that the Atlanteans built tunnel systems all over the world for various purposes. Firstly, to protect themselves from the then very common onslaughts of nature in the form of seismic activity and floods, and secondly, as a protection if attacked from outer space.

Most of these fantastic tunnels were constructed in ways beyond our present capabilities. For years England and France have been talking about the idea of a Channel Tunnel. However, it seems that the ancients built the amazing tunnels of their era as a matter of course, and on a very large scale, for good and imperative reasons.

In the first chapter it was shown that large land masses existed in the Atlantic until comparatively recent geological times. Now, let us focus our searchlight on the very large corpus of legends, traditions and myths describing the cataclysmic events attending the submergence of these lands. Lest it be objected at the beginning that this kind of material is capable of diverse interpretation and, therefore, of little scientific worth, I would point out that had written records of the same events come down to our own day from the very year of the occurrences, those documents would not be regarded as fanciful or valueless, and would be highly treasured items in some great library. (Plato's account was written some 9,000 years after the event.)

The very nature and scope of the catastrophe precluded the possibility of the survivors being in the happy position to sit down and write a history of the upheaval. Their sole occupation was to 'survive', and most of their energies were directed at finding or building suitable habitations, growing or finding food and reorganizing their existence.

In *Men Among Mankind*, referring to this terrible catastrophe, I wrote:

The population of the world after this series of catastrophes was very small. Those that were left had been driven almost insane and reduced to a state where they were little more than terrified animals. They never knew when another violent paroxysm of the earth might occur, causing hot lava to erupt out of cavities, tidal waves to overwhelm them or earthquakes to swallow them up.

Most of the survivors, because of the state of their minds, and the hopelessness for some time after the catastrophe of trying to establish themselves in any particular place, wandered

about the earth seeking their food wherever it could be found
... They were reduced to a wandering, hunting and fishing
state.[1]

Therefore, there can scarcely have been many oppor-
tunities to have put pen to paper or hammer to stone
(assuming that the survivors had such luxuries with them)
and to have prepared a written account of the great event.
Most of the survivors, shocked and preoccupied with maintaining their own existence, probably could not even write –
although a system of writing is known to have existed in
antediluvian times – and thus, through a combination of
these circumstances, memories of the terrible calamity
which had befallen early man and his animal companions
was transmitted to posterity in the form of oral traditions
and legends.

Colonel A. Braghine, whom we have mentioned previously, in *The Shadow of Atlantis*, observed on this
matter:

The French scientist Glotz speaks in his *History of Greece*
of the role of myths in historical research as follows: 'It is a
well-known fact that legend comes before history, but an
attentive and rigorous analysis of any myth gives us the oppor-
tunity to detect historical data even in a myth. The comparative method is very useful in these cases.'[2]

Adopting this procedure, I now intend to cite a large
number of legends which can only refer to the 'great catastrophe' which brought the Pleistocene period to an end.

In Dr. H. H. Bancroft's five-volumed treatise, *The Native
Races of the Pacific States of North America*, we find the
following information. The pre-Columbian tribes of Nicar-
agua, the Guatemalan Mixtecs, the Pimas and the
Papagos, all possessed a legend of a world deluge. The
Mattoles, a tribe of California, regard Taylor Peak as the
point on which their forefathers took refuge from a great
and destructive flood; the Chiperoyans say the deluge
covered all the earth, except the highest mountain tops

upon which many people were saved; while the Thlinkeets relate that many people accepted the deluge by seeking shelter in a great floating building.[3] This, of course, has great interest when compared with Noah's Ark in Genesis. However, there are many similar stories from all over the world relating to this catastrophic period.

A Brazilian deluge legend, describing how all humanity, excepting one man and his sister, was drowned, was mentioned by an unknown Portuguese chronicler who visited South America about A.D. 1590. The work is called *A Treatize on Brazil, written by a Portugall which had long lived there*, but it is referred to in *Hakluytus Posthumus, or Purchas His Pilgrimes, Contayning a History of the World in Sea Voyages and Lande Travels by Englishmen and Others*, by Samuel Purchas.[4]

In the Old World there are numerous deluge legends. One is connected with the myth of the hero Dardanos, who is reported to have crossed the Troad on a raft at the time of that event.[5]

The Greek hero Deucalion and his wife, Pyrrha, survived the Deluge – and he was subsequently known as 'the hero of the Universal Flood'.[6]

One of the best collections of traditions relating to the catastrophe is that found in H. S. Bellamy's book, *Moons, Myths and Man: A Reinterpretation*.

Bellamy wrote:

Less universal than the deluge myths, though not less striking, are the reports of a Great Fire which swept over the Earth as part of the great cosmic catastrophe which also caused the Great Flood...[7]

Bellamy then tells us that the Ntlakapamuk or Thompson River Indians, now settled in the Thompson River region of British Columbia in Canada, speak of a time when their ancestors witnessed a tremendous flood which quenched a Great Fire that raged over the world.[8]

The Gros Ventres tribe of Montana say that the god

Nichant destroyed the world first through fire and then through water. Another of these myths describes how the flood was sent to quench a great fire which had charred all the world.[9]

The Cato Indians of California say the Old World was bad and needed re-creating. Accordingly, the mountains were set on fire. The 'thunder-god', who lives in the world above, extinguished the conflagration with a flood of hot water. Then it began to rain night and day until the waters covered the greater part of the earth. The Wintun Indians of the Sacramento area of California have a legend in which it is said that when the god Katkochila had his 'magic flint' stolen, he sent, in his wrath, a Great Fire from the heavens which burnt all the earth. Then, he poured down a Great Flood to put out the fire.

The Washo Indians, another Californian tribe, tell of a great terrestrial revolution which caused the mountains to blaze up in flames so high that even the stars melted and fell on Earth. Then the sierras rose up from the plains, while other parts of the country were inundated.

This sequence of events is exactly that called for by modern geology, the youthful origin of most of the world's mountain systems being fully attested to by modern geological discoveries. Additionally, Immanuel Velikovsky has already been quoted in an earlier chapter on this point. (See also R. F. Flint's work, *Glacial Geology and the Pleistocene Epoch* – Author.)[10]

In South America, the Arawaks of Guyana (formerly British Guiana) say that the wickedness of antediluvian mankind was so dreadful that the Creator, Aiomun Kondi, who lives in heaven, twice ordered a general destruction; first, he scourged the world with fire, then he flooded it with water. A few men, however, contrived to escape both catastrophes, finding refuge from the fall of fiery rain in *underground caverns*, while at the time of the great flood, the ancestral Arawak chief Marerewana and his followers were able to escape in a canoe.[11]

Ignatius Donnelly, in his *Ragnarok: The Age of Fire and Gravel,* quoted the following British legend:

The profligacy of mankind had provoked the great Supreme to send a pestilential wind upon the earth. A pure poison descended, every blast was death. At this time the patriarch, distinguished for his integrity, was shut, together with his select company, in the enclosure within the strong door. (The cave?) Here the just ones were safe from injury. Presently the tempest of fire arose. It split the earth asunder to the great deep. The lake Llion burst its bounds, and the waves of the sea lifted themselves on high around the borders of Britain, the rain poured down from heaven, and the waters covered the earth.[12]

A very early Irish legend, mentioned by R. H. Mottram in his book *Noah,* refers to the flood:

One hundred and fifty women and three men led by Banba (one of the ancient poetical names given to Ireland) landed in Ireland before the flood. After they had been forty years on the land, a plague fell on them so that they all died within a week. Two hundred years after that Erin was a desert, empty without anyone alive in it ... After that came the Flood.[13]

It is remarkably significant that the number 40 in the above legend is assigned as the length of the pre-plague period in Ireland, especially as the same figure occurs frequently in legends from other sources describing, or in some way associated with, the Deluge, as in Genesis; moreover, it is curious that knowledge of Banba's Irish colony should have come down to us if, as we are told, all its members died of plague and Ireland was destitute of human beings for 200 years. Perhaps this particular legend has got a little of the old Blarney in it! The number 40, like the numbers 3 and 7, always was invested by the ancients with special magical or sacred significance.

Mottram mentioned numerous Deluge traditions in which a recognizable equivalent of Noah is to be found. For example, in a Hindu version, Mottram said that the sacred

Vedas were stolen by the giant Hayagrivah, an act which brought a universal deluge. Before the arrival of the flood, however, the good king Satyaorata – the Hindu deluge hero – was told by the god Vishnu to expect a ship which would come in time to save him and his court.

Mottram wrote:

In this case the rain came first – for seven days – and then, on the crest of the flood, already mounting, appeared the fabulous and ready-to-hand ship, and in this case alone there is some attempt to account for the means of propulsion, and it is a characteristically Eastern account. The god Vishnu came in the form of a fish, a million miles long, with an immense horn, to which the pious king made the ship fast. Then it was drawn for many years (a night of Brahma) and at length landed upon the highest peak of Mount Hunavan.[14]

Mottram compared this last account with several ancient Egyptian equivalents of Noah and the flood, and recorded that in the ancient Babylonian narrative Noah is called Hasisadra or Xisuthrus, the tenth king of the old Babylonian 'King-lists'. Ancient pre-Columbian equivalents of Noah listed by Mottram were Coxcox, Teocipactli and Tezpi.

Concerning Tezpi, M. Chadourne, in his interesting book *Anahuac: A Tale of a Mexican Journey*, wrote:

... At that time the waters covered the earth. Then Tezpi, as they called him, escaped on a boat full of all sorts of animals and creatures. After a long time he let loose a vulture. But it did not return – it stayed to feed on the dead bodies of giants, revealed by the falling waters. Then a humming bird, a Huitzitzila, was sent out, and it brought back a branch in its beak.[15]

The foregoing story certainly shows very great similarities to the Genesis narrative of Noah and the Flood.

Some interesting South American flood traditions were collected in 1572 by Sarmiento de Gamboa, who, referring to some pre-Incan accounts, wrote:

The Incas believed that, after the creation, Ticci-Viracocha sent a great flood to punish the sins of the first men, but the ancestors of the Cuzcos and some other nations were saved and so left some descendants. When the flood was over, Viracocha suddenly appeared on the Titicaca plateau with his servants, to help restore mankind and give them light.[16]

M. F. Denis recorded a Brazilian legend as long ago as 1550, when, in *Une Fête Brasilienne Célébré à Rouen en 1550*, he wrote:

Monan, without beginning or end, author of all that is, seeing the ingratitude of men, and their contempt for him who had made them thus joyous, withdrew from them, and sent upon them tata, the divine fire, that burned all that was on the surface of the Earth. He swept about the fire in such a way that in places he raised mountains, and in others dug valleys. Of all men one alone, Irin Mage, was saved, whom Monan carried into heaven. He, seeing all things destroyed, spoke thus to Monan: 'Wilt thou also destroy the heavens and their garniture? Alas! henceforth where will be our home? Why should I live, since there is none other of my kind?' Then Monan was so filled with pity that he poured a deluging rain on the Earth, which quenched the fire, and flowed on all sides, forming the oceans, which we call the parana, the great waters.[17]

This cataclysmic event extended all over the world. A Chinese account, published many years ago by Padre Martin Martinius in his *History of China*, reads:

... The pillars of heaven were broken. The Earth shook to its foundations. The sky sank lower towards the north. The sun, moon and stars changed their motions. The Earth fell to pieces, and the waters in its bosom uprushed with violence and overflowed ... The system of the universe was totally discorded. Man had rebelled against the high gods. The sun went into eclipse, the planets altered their courses, and the grand harmony of nature was disturbed.[18]

In the early part of this chapter I stated that I was going to adopt the comparative method, advocated by the French scientist Glotz, cited by Braghine, to detect historical data in myths. A large number of instances have been given from different parts of the world, all telling much the same story, that a terrible catastrophe overtook the planet in antediluvian times, bringing in some areas fire, followed by widespread floods causing most of the population to be wiped out. In many of these stories, as you have seen, certain good people were saved, and many of the tales have similarities to the Genesis narrative. It would seem that as a result of following the comparative method, when all these world-wide incidents are considered, and all these myths and legends taken into account (and there are very, very many more), historical data can be perceived. A world-wide catastrophe most certainly did take place.

As to the myths and legends themselves, it is hardly possible to improve on the summary of their value and importance published in 1887 by Sir Henry H. Howorth in his book, *The Mammoth and the Flood*:

> ... I do not profess to have collected all the deluge legends occurring among all races, but only a sufficient number to show how widespread the tradition is, and in how many shapes it occurs, showing that it is not due to its having spread from a common focus, but that the stories are independent ... I do not want to exaggerate the importance of this kind of testimony. I only place it alongside of that which I have adduced from another field altogether, to show how consistent along the whole line the evidence is, induction from palaeontology and archaeology compelling the same conclusion as the legendary myths and stories of the scattered children of men. All point unmistakably, it seems to me, to a widespread catastrophe, involving a flood on a great scale ...[19]

There are many references in classic mythology, the Bible, and the folk-lore of various races, to an underworld, variously called Hades, Hell and Tartarus. It is my contention that this lower world is very real and physical, and its occupants exert a tremendous influence upon surface dwellers today.

At this stage, I wish to bring to your attention the many attempts to manufacture different forms of life in Tartarus by a mad scientist, no less a person than Satan; sometimes called Satanaku or Pluto.

You will recall that, after defeating the Titans, Zeus had to contend with the Giants. According to mythology they had been conceived from the blood of the mutilated Uranus. In an earlier chapter I mentioned that some ideas would be given about this.

Those giants were terrible mutants with reptilian legs and feet consisting of serpent heads. They had many other unpleasant features which need not be enlarged upon here. I think that it is already quite plain that they were not exactly the sort of people you would like to meet socially.

It seems to me that over the very long passage of time this story has come down to us in a distorted form, though the implication comes through quite clearly, taking into account other examples of 'abominations' being manufactured in Tartarus. In short, when mythology relates that those giants were conceived from the blood of the mutilated Uranus, this is another way of telling us those horrible mutants were made in the underworld of Tartarus.

We have already referred to the story of the monster, Typhoeus, that 'Gaea had borne to Tartarus', which is a clear indication that it was made by Satanic forces in the underground caverns of Satanaku.

Harold T. Wilkins, in his *Secret Cities of Old South America*, quoting from the remarkable book *El Daoud*, wrote:

... In Atlan, the secret caverns of Satanaku were filled with abominations created by his awful wickedness. The lowlands of Atlantis were thoroughly infected and infested with black magic, and the sacred heights were no longer needed for the Elders, or Dhuman-Adamics ... It was the magic of yellow, red and black rebels...[1]

There is really no such thing as 'magic'. What is termed 'magic' consists of a series of unusual manipulations of natural forces or laws, known only to a few initiates. The results, highly extraordinary from the point of view of the vast, ignorant masses, were duly thought of as supernatural or 'magical'.

There are reasons for thinking that the Devil or Satan was a Titan. Since we know that Isis, wife of Ra and of Osiris, was, with other contemporaries, reputedly versed in all medical cures, and is even credited with performing elaborate surgery to restore the slain Osiris to a further, though limited span of life, it does not seem beyond the bounds of reason to suppose that this medical knowledge was also possessed by the Titans. That being so, it is also reasonable to suppose that the Titans, and perhaps Satan (Satanaku), who may have been especially interested in surgery and medicine, carried out medical experiments. Such experiments would have been far beyond the ken of the mass of humanity in those times and would accordingly have been considered 'magic'.

In the late 1920s, Waldemar Julsrud discovered in Mexico thousands of figurines ranging in height from two inches to six feet, buried deep under sand and volcanic lava. He spent the next twenty years digging up some 66,000 of these fantastic figurines.

Many of these figurines were of snakes, giraffes and

other animals. However, a large percentage were of hybrid forms. Some of them depicted beings that were half human and half animal. Others were of monsters devouring humans; some pictured giants tearing the limbs off humans.

The Julsrud figurines have been examined by many scientists, including Professor Charles H. Hapgood, mentioned earlier, and are known to date from more than 9,000 years ago.

The figurines have been modelled very carefully, and are so realistic that they must have been based upon actual events and experiments that were taking place at the time, or in very recent memory of the unknown artists. Most of them are highly malevolent. (A friend of mine, Mr. J. B. Delair, was in touch with the late Waldemar Julsrud, who gave him some of the figurines. I have seen a few myself and can vouch for their bestial and horrible realistic appearance – Author.)

The discovery of this vast number of figurines is surely very strong proof of what went on in Satanaku's underground caverns.

Were the 'abominations' in secret caverns of Old Atlan by Satanaku attempts at surgery gone wrong, or endeavours to create some new kinds of life? Was the manufacture by Satan of a new form of creature the cause of his pride? Had he achieved perhaps, in horrific form, what nobody else, not even Zeus, had managed before?

How else can the facts – wild and scattered as some of them are – be rationally explained? Remember too, that vivisection and diabolical surgery were conducted on animals and human beings by Nazi fanatics within living memory.

After the final cataclysm horrific monsters appeared from the bowels of the earth, probably because seismic activity smashed some of the subterranean caverns, and these terrible creatures escaped to the surface. These are mentioned in Greek mythology and they were finally destroyed by 'The Heroes'.

Those monsters killed by such Heroes as Herakles, Jason, Bellerophon, Cadmus, Theseus, Beowolf, Sigurd and others, all seem to have been (1) unique in form, and (2) relatively few in number.

There are, at least, some grounds for believing that Satan was possibly a medical scientist, fanatical to an impossible degree by present day thinking in his desire to manufacture new forms of life. He would go to any extremes in order to achieve his ends. In short, though he undoubtedly had god-like powers, on the basis of what I have just written, he was a mad scientist.

H. E. Guerber, in his book *The Myths of Greece and Rome*, describes the ruler of Tartarus in these words:

Pluto is always represented as a stern, dark, bearded man, with tightly closed lips, a crown on his head, a sceptre and a key in hand, to show how carefully he guards those who enter his domain and how vain are their hopes to effect an escape. No temples were dedicated to him, and statues of this god are very rare. Human sacrifices were sometimes offered on his altars; and at his festivals held every hundred years, and thence called Secular Games, none but black animals were slain.

His kingdom, generally called Hades, was very difficult of access ...[2]

Traditionally, Hades had four rivers flowing through it, and further reference to these will be made later in this book. Guerber names them as the Styx, the Acheron, the Phlegeton and the Cocytus.

The great poet Alighieri Dante (A.D. 1265–1321), in his major work the *Commedia*, which is now known as the *Divine Comedy*, relates how he was escorted by Virgil through the two lower worlds, Hell and Purgatory.

An article in *The Encyclopaedia Britannica* referring to Dante's description of Hell stated: 'Hell is conceived as a vast conical hollow, reaching to the centre of the earth ...'[3]

This is very interesting, in view of what will be put forward in the next part of the book as proof for a hollow

Earth. It is not suggested by this author that Dante actually descended into the centre of the Earth. The *Divine Comedy* is a great imaginative poem in which the poet plays a leading role himself. However, it does show how engrained on the minds of the ancients, even the early Christians, was the concept of Hell or Hades, situated in the centre of the Earth.

Another interesting point concerns Jesus. It will be recalled that according to the Bible, just prior to his ascension, Jesus descended into Hell.

There is no doubt that the ancient Greeks and other nations believed in an actual, real, physical underworld. Later on, theologists regarded it as a non-physical place you might be despatched to after death, instead of Heaven, if you did not come up to scratch.

It is the purpose of this book to prove that this underworld really existed, and still does today. Once again, there is no smoke without fire, and I believe that there is a lot of smoke.

Before Poseidonis, the last great island of Atlantis, sank beneath the waves, the old Empire of the Sun had lost its original stature and the great civilization had degenerated through the use of black magic.

Some of the Atlanteans may have escaped in space ships; others had gone eastwards and westwards away from the mother country, hoping to escape from the catastrophe, and survived on the surface to give us our present civilization. Most of them, however, took refuge in the tunnel systems connecting with the hollow Earth, and their descendants are still there, today, living in fabulous cities inside our planet.

All this may sound incredible to us mundane surface dwellers. Nevertheless, in the next part of this book proof will be given that the Earth is really hollow. *Fasten your seat belts for a flight into the centre of the Earth through the polar entrance!*

Part Two   The Case for a Hollow Earth

9 : Legends of the Inner World

In my first book, *The Sky People*, the original Garden of Eden was placed on another planet.[1]

You will recall that after the 'Fall' Adam was expelled from Eden.

> Therefore the Lord God sent him
> forth from the Garden of Eden,
> to till the ground *from whence he was taken.*
>
> Genesis 3 : 23
> (italics mine – Author)

In that early book it was postulated that a number of the Elchim (gods) had indulged in a breeding experiment. This went wrong and they were expelled, too, along with the race of Adam. These were the 'fallen angels'.

Now, where was the first earthly Garden of Eden?

William F. Warren, in his scholarly work *Paradise Found, or The Cradle of the Human Race at the North Pole*, quotes from a translation by A. M. Sayce taken from a book called *Records of the Past*:

We are told of a dwelling which 'the gods created for' the first human beings – a dwelling in which 'they became great', and 'increased in numbers', and the location of which is described in words exactly corresponding to those of Iranian, Indian, Chinese, Eddaic and Aztecan literature; namely, 'in the centre of the Earth'.[2]

Warren places the entrance to this Paradise firmly and squarely in the North Polar area.

There are many biblical references to this area. Here is a very pertinent one from *Job*:

He stretcheth out the north over
the empty place, and hangeth
the earth upon nothing.
He bindeth up the waters in his
thick clouds; and the cloud is not rent
under them.
He holdeth back the face of his
throne, and spreadeth his cloud upon it.
He hath encompassed the waters with
bounds until the day and night come
to an end.

Job 26: 7–10

An American who has done considerable research into the hollow Earth theory is Raymond A. Palmer, a magazine editor and publisher.

In an article Palmer commented upon these verses from *Job*:

Viewed from space, the Earth would seem to be spherical, and the hole would not in any way change the regularity of the sphere. (We will be discussing the hole later – Author.) We can easily understand this when Job makes his reiterated mentions of the clouds that cover the hole (polar explorers curse the eternal fog). Particularly in 'he holdeth back the face of his throne, and spreadeth his cloud upon it'.[3]

The Scandinavians have a legend of a wonderful land far to the north called Ultima Thule (often confused today with Greenland). Is Ultima Thule in that mysterious area *beyond* the Pole alleged to lead into the interior of the Earth?

The well-known French writer, Robert Charroux, has written of the legends of the underground worlds of Agartha and Shamballah.[4]

There are many more references both in the Bible and in classical literature to this legendary inner world.

Now we will present real, solid proof that the Earth, without any doubt whatsoever, is hollow.

10 :   The Conditions are Favourable

William Reed pointed out at the start of his book, *The Phantom of the Poles*, that the Earth is round and flattened at the poles. At the time he wrote his work it was probably not realized that the Earth is spherical, rather·than round.
He wrote:

If now we can produce enough other evidence to prove that the Earth is double, then we have shown why it is flattened at the poles. The fact that the Earth is flattened at the poles is not any proof that the Earth is double, or hollow. *It only shows that the shape of the Earth is not only favourable to such a condition, but absolutely necessary and gives a good foundation with which to start.*[1] (italics mine – Author)

The basis of Marshall B. Gardner's theme was that all nebulae evolve towards a certain form. That *all* planets, including our own, are hollow with entrances at the poles, and with a central sun.

Gardner suggested that the phenomenon known as the *aurora borealis* is really a reflection coming through the north polar entrance of the central sun in the interior.

He pointed to the observations of the polar caps of Mars, Venus and other planets, and to the luminosity that was seen in those areas, which was from the central suns inside those planets:

A snow cap would not reflect light with so much more vividness than the other surfaces of the planet, and only direct beams of light coming from a central sun could give that luminous effect above the surface of the planet and varying as the atmosphere in the interior or above was clouded or clear. Had it been a mere ice cap there would not have been this luminosity, and, in particular, there would have been no luminosity when the planet was covered with clouds as Lockyer says it was. Furthermore, that luminosity is precisely what our own *aurora borealis* would look like if our planet was viewed from a great distance. And the light is the same in both cases.[2]

It is interesting that the Van Allen belts, zones of intense radiation surrounding the Earth, which were discovered a few years ago, have gaps at both polar areas. Soon after their discovery, an article about the belts appeared in the *Scientific American*, complete with drawings of their shape.

Palmer wrote in his magazine, commenting on this article:

Especially note the drawings of its shape, which are precisely a vast 'doughnut', with the spherical Earth pictured at its centre, in the 'hole' of the doughnut. What if the Earth is not spherical, but actually doughnut-shaped, exactly as its surrounding Van Allen Belt? Whatever makes the belt thusly shaped, might it not also be responsible for shaping the earth similarly? ...

Aimé Michel, in his straight line theory, proved that most of the 'flight patterns' of the flying saucers are on a north–south course, which is exactly what would be true if the origin of the saucers is polar.[3,4]

Aimé Michel is a very well known French writer on UFOs, and highly respected in the field of UFO research.

Now, what is the accepted scientific thinking on the structure of the Earth today? This obviously is most important. It had been generally accepted for a very long time that the Earth had a fluid, molten core. Geologists no longer hold to this view. They do not accept that the Earth is hollow, either. Nevertheless, over the years they have changed their views, as scientists are prone to do.

The Institute of Geological Sciences in London kindly sent the author a summary of the current thought on the Earth's interior.

The Institute stated:

The Earth's interior has a layered structure: the outermost layer is the crust; beneath is the mantle, and then the core. Scientists cannot study the interior of the Earth directly. What we know of it is worked out from studying the way earthquake waves are bent as they pass through the Earth...

The Earth's core is a dense material, probably iron with some dissolved sulphur and silicon. The outer core behaves as a liquid, but the inner core is a *solid*. The Earth's magnetic field is generated by circulation movements in the liquid outer core.[5] (italics mine – Author)

Well, at any rate, the aforementioned material indicates that we have got rid of the old liquid molten core concept! The fact that they now think the inner core is a solid is another tremendous step forward for our case. *The centre of the Earth would have to be made of solid material for it eventually to be proved hollow!*

Now, let us take a look at the way Nature operates. Everything, including bones, hair and stalks of plants is hollow. A Geode stone is hollow. So, why not planets? After all, a planet is a living body.

A scientist, Dr. Orville Livingston Leech, stated:

The possibilities of a land inside the Earth were first brought to my attention when I picked up a geode on the shores of The Great Lakes. The geode is a spherical and apparently solid stone, but when broken is found to be hollow and coated with crystals. The Earth is only a larger form of a geode, and the law that created the geode in its hollow form undoubtedly fashioned the Earth in the same way.

Gardner postulated that all nebulae in space are hollow. Furthermore he stated that comets (which in his view were dead planets) were also hollow, and in his book included a fascinating photographic reproduction of a drawing showing the head of Donati's Comet as seen from Cambridge University on 1 October, 1853. The caption that appeared under the picture is well worth including here:

The Central nucleus is very plainly seen, surrounded by a

sphere of glowing gases, and enclosed by an outer envelope. The comet is passing through an area of conflicting forces, and this, and perhaps the excessive heat of the body, has caused the great split which extends through the envelope to the central sun itself. A comet is simply a planet which is disintegrating, and the photograph shows us the disintegration taking place, and just far enough advanced so that we can see the inner structure of the planet. And that structure is precisely what our theory says is the actual structure of all planets, our Earth included . . .[6]

We have here a tremendous concept. That everything, including nebulae, comets and planets, is hollow, along with everything in Nature. This is certainly food for thought. *The conditions for a hollow Earth are indeed favourable.*

11 :   Has the North Pole been Reached?

An essential part of our case it that there is no North Pole. No single point, but instead a big area which is a warm sea dipping gradually into the interior of the Earth. This may sound incredible but we will be presenting strong evidence to support this idea in the next few pages.

At this stage many of you will be thinking about those polar explorers who claimed to have reached the North Pole.

The first point to make is that compasses go completely haywire in the Arctic Circle. A very competent, honest and famous Norwegian explorer, Dr. Fridtjof Nansen, on his expedition to try and reach the North Pole in 1895, lost his bearings and freely admitted that he had not the slightest idea where he was for a very long period.

In February, 1895, after landing from the vessel *Fram*, Nansen set off on a northward sledge journey which he hoped would take him to the Pole and from there to Spitzbergen by way of Franz Joseph Land.

From 29 March, 1895, until the spring of 1896 the Norwegian explorer was completely lost!

Furthermore, to his astonishment he discovered that after journeying through cold regions *the weather began to get warmer*. He noticed that whenever the wind blew from the north, the temperature began to rise. At one time the sun became unbearably hot! Imagine that in the polar regions!

Nansen took soundings and found that the depth of the polar water was very much greater than had been previously thought. He was surprised to find out how warm the water was at great depth. He did not know from where this warm water emanated!

Then he came across animals that according to accepted knowledge should not have been in those regions.

On 26 April, 1895, Nansen wrote:

I was not a little surprised yesterday morning when I suddenly saw the track of an animal in the snow. It was that of a fox, came about W.S.W. true, and went in an easterly direction. The trail was quite fresh. What in the world was the fox doing up here? There were also unequivocal signs that it had not been without food. Were we in the vicinity of land? I looked around for it, but the weather was thick all day yesterday, and we might have been near it without seeing it. In any case a warm-blooded mammal in the eighty-fifth parallel. We had not gone far before we came across another fox track, it went in about the same direction as the other, and followed the trend of the lane which had stopped us and by which we had been obliged to camp. It is incomprehensible what these animals live on up here, but presumably they are able to snap up some crustaceans in the open waterways. But why do they leave the coasts? That is what puzzles me most. Can they have gone astray? There seems little probability of that.[1]

To sum up the experiences of Nansen so far.

(1) He was lost for a period from early 1895 to late spring, 1896, a fact he freely admitted throughout that time.

(2) The further north he went the warmer it became, and at one point the weather was really scorching. On 16 April, 1895, 'the sun scorched quite unpleasantly. The tent was pitched in broiling sun, and for days after the atmosphere was equable and stagnant.'

(3) He saw the trails of foxes. Warm-blooded animals that should not have been in those areas.

Now, what are we to make of all this? It is not proof, but is some kind of evidence that the warm weather, the warm water and the animals might conceivably come from a hollow Earth through a polar entrance.

It occurred to me that during the International Geophysical Year, 1957–8, a tremendous amount of exploratory and research work was carried out by scientists of many nations in both polar areas, and that these activities have been continued ever since.

I therefore decided to write to the Scott Polar Research Institute at Cambridge, who are *the* people on polar research. In my letter I brought to their notice the astonished remarks of Nansen upon finding the fox trails on the ice pack so far north, and also asked them to comment on the warm winds coming from the north; the broiling sun which he and his companion had to put up with for some days and, finally, the warm sea that they eventually reached.

My letter addressed to the Director of the Institute, was passed to their Librarian, who kindly replied on 5 November, 1973, as follows:

Dear Mr. Le Poer Trench,

Thank you for your letter of 26 October. There is a considerable mammalian wildlife population in the Arctic, including Arctic Fox, Arctic Rabbit, lemmings, polar bear etc. Only the latter spends much of its life hunting on the frozen pack, though as Nansen indicates other creatures occasionally stray from land proper on to the sea ice. The subject is dealt with admirably by Bernard Stonehouse in his book *Animals of the Arctic; the Ecology of the Far North*, London, Ward Lock, 1971. This book also contains useful chapters dealing with climate etc. If after consulting this book you find yourself with additional queries I would suggest paying a visit to our extremely well-stocked library of books and periodicals.

Yours sincerely,
H. G. R. King
Librarian.

Although the Institute informed me about animal life in the Arctic, they did not comment on Nansen's very surprised remarks on finding the fox trails. After all, he was no novice at polar exploration.

My other questions were not directly answered at all. Instead, I was referred to a book. I obtained this recommended work. It is a splendid affair with superb colour pictures of the Arctic animals, but on consulting the chapters on climate and the Arctic Ocean, I drew a complete blank in regard to Nansen's experiences.

Naturally, I am appreciative of the information supplied by the Scott Polar Research Institute, but it is surprising that they did not comment directly on Nansen's account of the warm winds coming from the north, the broiling sun for days on end and the warm sea. I would have thought that these most unusual experiences undergone by the great Norwegian explorer would have been of very special interest to them.

We now come to an extremely important part of our case. I refer to the behaviour of the compass needle in the polar regions. If we assume for the moment that the polar entrance is there, when you are entering the curve of the Earth, that is going down into the interior, the magnetic pole pulls one end of the needle up, toward a perpendicular position.

When you are travelling down instead of horizontally on the Earth's surface, and are entering the interior, the needle must point up, towards the north magnetic pole, rather than north, as it did when travelling on the Earth's horizontal surface. I hope that you are with me, as this is rather important.

This is what happened to Nansen! He wrote, referring to Johansen, his assistant:

One day, it was 24 November, he came in to supper a little after six o'clock, quite alarmed and said, 'There has just been a singular inclination of the needle to twenty-four degrees and, remarkably enough, its northern extremity pointed to the east. I cannot remember ever having heard of such an inclination.'[2]

If Nansen had still been on the surface of the Earth, his position at that time probably would have put the compass on an angle of forty-five degrees, if not more.

At this point, it is interesting to mention a race of people on the surface of the Earth that may play a role in our searches for the truth. The Eskimos.

The Eskimos inhabit the Arctic coast of America from Greenland to Alaska and part of the Asiatic side of the Bering Strait. Some of them are found very far north near the polar regions hunting the seal and other animals.

It has already been mentioned that the further north you go the colder it becomes, then as some polar explorers have discovered the weather becomes milder, finally almost unbearably hot, and a warm sea is reached.

This is a very important part of our case. The Eskimos are a people who have kept very much to themselves, for the most part friendly, but are hunters and prone to get fat through eating a lot of raw flesh. They are not a tall people, with mostly flat noses and oblique set eyes, but are intelligent and good humoured.

Now, I come to the real point about the Eskimos. In his book, Gardner states that the 'Eskimo who came too far south found out what we have seen that the polar explorers from our own countries found out – a greater abundance of life further north'.[3]

This may seem strange, but we have already mentioned how Nansen came across animals that according to accepted thinking should not have been there.

Gardner wrote:

That the Eskimo came from the interior of the Earth, that is to say, from a location which they could not easily explain to the Norwegians who might have asked them where they originally came from, is shown by the fact that the early Norwegians regarded them as a supernatural people, a species of fairy.[4]

He went on to quote from the second volume of Dr. Nansen's work *In Northern Mists*:

I have already stated that the Norse name 'Skraeling' for Eskimo must have originally been used as a designation of fairies or mythical creatures. Furthermore, there is much that would imply that when the Icelanders first met with the Eskimo in Greenland they looked upon them as fairies; they, therefore, called them 'trolls', an ancient common name for various sorts of supernatural beings . . .[5]

We will now discuss the respective claims of Dr. Frederick A. Cook and Admiral Robert Edwin Peary to have reached the North Pole.

Cook claimed to have been the first man to reach the North Pole on 21 April, 1908. His claim to have forestalled Peary was at first credited, 'and he was given a rapturous reception at Copenhagen, but scientific opinion in England and America was more reserved, and eventually, after a prolonged dispute, a special committee of the University of Copenhagen, to whom his documents were submitted, declared that they contained no proof that he had reached the Pole. By that time most other people had come to an adverse opinion and the sensation was over'.[6]

Cook had with him two Eskimos who knew nothing about determining latitudes or longitudes, and the notes he produced were not sufficient evidence to support his claim to have reached the Pole.

Now, we come to the claims of Admiral Peary to have reached the North Pole on 6 April, 1909. An interesting point is that Peary sent back all his white companions a few days' march from the Pole, and pushed forward alone with his Negro servant and two Eskimos. As in the case of Cook, the whole business relies entirely on the word of Peary alone. Those that were with him had no knowledge of taking bearings as to their positions.

Peary took even fewer observations of his claimed position at the Pole than Cook had done. Furthermore, whereas Cook was challeged on his claims to have travelled 15 miles a day, Peary stated that he did some 20 to 40 miles a day, actually 40 miles on one day, and remember that he and those with him were pushing their sledge through Arctic ice.

Although Peary's word was at first accepted and the world acknowledged the Pole had been reached, when his proofs were submitted for investigation, the committee stated that he had not proved his point.

I must say, here and now, though it seems likely from the investigations of the various committees concerned that probably both Cook and Peary did not reach the North Pole (which, according to our case, does not exist), tribute should be paid to both these fine explorers. No doubt, both explorers really thought they had reached the Pole.

Dr. George Tittman, who at the time of Cook and Peary's expeditions was head of the coast and geodetic survey at Washington, made an interesting statement about what could be the actual physical conditions at the Pole.

He said:

There are really no scientific theories as to what is immediately around the Pole. There are some theorists who think that there is an open sea and some who think that a fertile spot is there. Scientific men are inclined to think that there may be little difference in immediate conditions close to the Pole from those in the Arctic regions miles from there.[7]

This is an amazing statement coming from a scientist, even though it is from one who has now left us.

Now, you will recall the statements quoted earlier from the honest and competent explorer, Nansen, regarding the warm sea, the warm weather and trails of warm-blooded animals, the further north he went.

It is our thesis that there is an open sea in the area where the Pole is supposed to be, because all explorers who have gone far enough north have found one.

A most significant fact is that polar explorers who have journeyed some distance on the warm sea, including Nansen, found *that there was a very gradual foreshortening of the horizon from north to south, while the east–west distance remained constant.*

Surely, this indicated that the warm sea descends into the interior of the Earth. That 'Land *Beyond* the Pole' that Admiral Byrd spoke about and which we will be discussing later.

12 : The Russians are on to it!

It would seem that some years ago the Russians were trying to let a little of the proverbial 'cat out of the bag' about
the mysteries of the North Polar area.

An article in the *Scientific American* pointed out that the
Russians have discarded the idea of a single point at the
North Magnetic Pole, and now say that it is not a point at
all, but a line approximately 1,000 miles long! They have,
also, discovered much else, as you will see in this chapter.[1]

Palmer, describing and commenting on the material in
the *Scientific American* article in his own magazine, wrote :

But now we have, available in the form of the records of
several hundred years, in Russian archives, a history of Arctic
exploration which proves our most important point beyond
any further question; i.e., that the Pole is not a point, but
(deduce the Russians) a 'line' approximately 1,000 miles long.
Before we go further, we might suggest that we think they are
wrong in this deduction, and that instead of being a line, it is
actually a circle, but because of the lack of space to place it on
the globe, the Russians have been forced to compress their
observations into the flattened-out state that a circle becomes
when compressed into a two-dimensional area. They had to
squeeze the circle from two sides and make a line of it. We'd
like to give you now a résumé of that single phase of Russian
exploration, which actually covered much more than just
geomagnetism.

Here is what the Russians say :

Navigators in the high latitudes have always been troubled
by the odd behaviour of their magnetic compasses caused by
apparent irregularities and asymmetries in the magnetic field
of the Earth. Early magnetic maps had been drawn on the
assumption, based upon hopeful guesses, that the North Mag-

netic Pole is virtually a point. Accordingly it was expected that the compass needle, which dips more steeply as it approaches the Magnetic Pole, would point straight down, or very nearly so, at the Magnetic Pole itself. But data from many Russian and other expeditions showed that the compass needle points straight down for a very long distance across the Arctic Ocean, from a point northwest of the Taimyr Peninsular to another point in the Arctic Archipelago. This discovery first inspired the hypothesis that there is a second North Magnetic Pole, tentatively located at 86 degrees East longitude. More refined observation has disposed of this idea. The map of the magnetic field now shows the magnetic meridians running close together in a thick bunch of lines from the North Magnetic Pole in the Arctic Archipelago to Siberia.

Geomagnetic studies, in co-ordination with the International Geophysical Year, have been extended to high altitudes. This work has clarified the interaction of the magnetic field with the charged particles emitted by the Sun, especially with respect to the formation of the belts of radiation that surround the earth, the generation of magnetic storms and the production of auroral displays. Today stations in the Arctic conduct regular simultaneous observations with stations in the Antarctic. Along with its great theoretical interest, the programme has given improved accuracy to navigation charts of the Arctic regions . . .

Exploration and research have shown that an enormous region of the Earth's surface and correspondingly large realms of the unknown may be brought within the compass of human understanding in a very few years. The data thus far amassed by expeditions and ice stations fill more than 120 volumes; the list of books, monographs and articles that is emerging from that data already exceeds 600 titles . . .

That concluded Palmer's résumé of the Russian scientific work in the Arctic from the *Scientific American* article. He went on:

Let's make some comments on the presented material, paragraph by paragraph. It is unnecessary to say much more about the geomagnetic readings which have established that the 'Pole', magnetically speaking, *is* a very extended area that crosses the Polar Basin from one continent to the other. It is at least 1,000 miles long, and more likely can be said to exist as a rather diffuse line for 1,000 more. Thus, when Admiral Peary (and other Arctic explorers who used a magnetic compass) claims to have 'reached' the Pole, he is making a very vague claim indeed. He can only say that he reached a point, which could be anywhere in a demonstrable 2,000 mile area, where his compass pointed straight down. A noteworthy achievement, but not a 'discovery of the Pole'...

Next, having found themselves stumped to account for the strange observations in the Polar Basin, the theorists have turned to space and the upper atmosphere and even to the Sun for an explanation of what is happening to their instruments. Now the 'Pole' is 'interaction of the magnetic field with charged particles from the Sun'...

This brings us to the subject of 'mystery lands' of great extent in the polar areas which cannot possibly be placed on our globe without overlapping seriously in impossible ways.

In the last two paragraphs of our quotation from the Russian data, we find much 'hidden inference', and we'll try to point it out to you. First, let's examine the quotation: 'Exploration and research have shown that an enormous region of the Earth's surface *and correspondingly large realms of the unknown may be brought within the compass of human understanding* in a very few years.' This is truly a stupendous sentence! (Italics mine – Author) Contemplate what it actually says:

It says that not only exploration, but 'research' have shown that enormous regions of the Earth's surface *and* corresponding (get that word, corresponding) large realms of the *unknown* may be brought into the compass of *understanding* of human beings in a very few years. In plain words, in addition to the areas we can understand and investigate by exploration, there are large realms which have to be brought to human understanding by means of research.

Oh yes, large *unknown* and even *beyond present understandability* areas do exist, and it 'may be' that we will discover and comprehend them in a very few years...

We might say that all this is double talk. We might also say secrets are being kept. But we won't. The fact is that neither is true. This is *straight* talk, the only kind of talk we can expect from anyone who is trying to tell something, but cannot because it is, as yet, beyond his understanding. To say definitely that there are large land masses inside an area commonly called a 'point' is to be faced with the challenge to explain and to demonstrate and prove. Since this cannot yet be done, the speaker is left rather helpless to do more than vaguely hint at mysteries ...

What is it that exists at both poles of the earth which opens to us new frontiers so vast in extent and nature as to be beyond present understanding? It may well be that the exploration of space is far less important than the exploration of our own mysterious planet, now suddenly become a 'vast realm' far larger than we have ever dreamed it to be.[2]

13: Commercial Flights over the Pole and Submarine Expeditions under it

A certain airline which claims flights daily 'over the Pole' does not come closer than 1,500 miles to the Geographic Pole, and not even within 250 miles of the Magnetic Pole. *It is because gyroscopic compasses don't work within 150 miles approximately of the Pole* and that is why advertised 'flights over the Pole' do not go anywhere near it.

No airline could afford to have its aircraft getting lost over the Polar area with all the consequent danger this would mean to the passengers.

This too, is why, military pilots are instructed to make direction changes when their instruments begin to go haywire, so that they can get back into an area where the gyroscope works.

Now, let us turn our searchlight on to the expeditions made to the Pole underwater by the submarines *Nautilus* and *Skate*. It was claimed that *Nautilus* went to the Pole, crossed it and then turned directly towards Spitzbergen. It did *not go straight* across the Pole and continue on *straight*.

The Pole is *never* crossed by military and commercial aircraft, unless it is a Byrd type flight (which we will be discussing later). They always play it safe and navigate so they won't get lost. And it is so very easy to get lost in the Arctic close to the Pole.

Why didn't *Nautilus* continue straight on after reaching the Pole? Why did the submarine veer off to Spitzbergen?

The reason is that prior to the polar trip '*Nautilus* had made an exploratory cruise under the ice pack in the autumn of 1957 and discovered there were problems. Her gyrocompasses had failed...' And again, 'By the next afternoon we (*Skate*) were within 150 miles of the Pole, and our regular gyrocompasses could no longer tell us which direction was north."[1]

Palmer, commenting on this situation, wrote:

So what did *Nautilus* and *Skate* use in navigating under the polar ice? Well, they invented a new use for a device originally designed as a guided missile gimcrack – the 'inertial guidance system'. They adapted it to submarine navigation.

In short, this system senses the Earth's rotation and charts its speed. Delicate instruments feel the direction of the motion resulting from the Earth's eastward spin, thus telling which direction is east. They sense speed as well as motion, and since the rotation of a point on the Earth's surface decreases as one goes towards the Poles, the inertial gadgets can sense their distance from the Poles...

We think *Nautilus* and *Skate* reached a point where the inertial guidance system showed no eastward motion of the Earth, but *it is merely an assumption that this lack of motion means the point reached is the Geographic North Pole.* All it means is that they reached a 'failure point' where the inertial guidance system no longer is able to determine motion, *just as the gyrocompass, at a distance of 150 miles from the Pole, is unable to decide when it is being swerved and not being swerved from its axis of rotation.*[2]

It seems that foolproof instruments to tell you that the Pole has been reached simply do not exist! We have shown that magnetic compasses, gyrocompasses, and maybe even inertial guidance systems are not foolproof.

Strange though it may seem, the likelihood is that no one has succeeded in reaching the North Pole. If our case is correct then the North Pole is not just a point, but located in the big polar entrance. It is probable that Nansen and some other polar explorers have gone some distance into the interior. It is possible, as we shall see later, that Admiral Richard E. Byrd flew 1,700 miles beyond the Pole to that 'enchanted continent in the sky'.

14: More Awkward Questions

There are a lot more questions that need good answers.
Here is awkward question number one.

*Why is there so much dust in the farthermost northern
areas of the Arctic?*

Many polar explorers have found this dust most dis-
agreeable. Nansen complained bitterly about it.

Let us go home! What have we to stay for? Nothing but
dust, dust, dust![1]

The profusion of dust in the Arctic floats in great clouds
and falls over ships – if they happen to be there – and
colours the snow black.

Where does all this dust come from? There are no active
volcanoes in the Arctic!

Reed wrote:

The next query is concerning the great quantities of dust
constantly found in the Arctic Ocean. What causes this dust?
The volcanic eruptions that send up the rocks called shooting
stars. One does not ask what this dust is composed of; for it
has been analysed, and found to be carbon and iron, supposed
to come out of some volcano.[2]

I repeat: Where is this volcano? There are none in the
Arctic Circle. However, if there was a burning volcano in
the interior of the Earth, great clouds and dust would come
up through the entrance, falling on to the snow and colouring it a nightmarish black.

This leads to our next question.

What causes coloured snow in the Arctic region?

We have already discussed the black snow caused by
clouds of dust. There is also the strange phenomenon of
red, pink, green, blue and yellow snow! This coloured snow

has also been analysed and found to contain vegetable matter, supposed to be the blossom or pollen of a plant.

No such plant is known to grow on the surface of the Earth!

Reed tells us:

The interior of the Earth is the only spot that will furnish us with an answer to the question. As the colours fall at different seasons, it is fair to presume that the flower matures at those seasons...

Kane, in his first volume, page 44, says, 'We passed the "Crimson Cliffs" of Sir John Ross in the forenoon of August 5th. The patches of red snow, from which they derive their name, could be seen clearly at the distance of ten miles from the coast. They had a fine, deep-rose hue, not at all like the brown stain which I noticed when I was here before. All the gorges and ravines in which the snow had lodged were deeply tinted with it. I had no difficulty now in justifying the somewhat poetical nomenclature which Sir John Franklin applied to this locality; for if the snowy surface were more diffused, as it is no doubt earlier in the season, crimson would be the prevailing colour.[3]

A flower that produces pollen in such profusion must need thousands of acres in which to grow!

If, as already stated, no such flower grows on Earth, then the pollen must be wafted up through the polar entrance from the interior. This could not happen unless the Earth is hollow and the warm air coming up from inside distributed the pollen over the Arctic region.

Next question, please.

If no rivers are flowing from the inside of the Earth to the outside, then why are all icebergs composed of fresh water?

Reed wrote:

Icebergs are next in order. Where are they formed? And how? In the interior of the Earth, where it is warm, by streams or canyons flowing to the Arctic Circle, where it is very cold, the mouth of the stream freezing and the water, continuing to pass over it, freezing as it flows. This prevails for months, until, owing to the warm weather in summer, the warmth from the Earth, and the warm rains passing down to the sea, the bergs are thawed loose and washed into the ocean. Icebergs cannot be formed on Earth, for the reason that it is colder inland than at the mouth of a stream; hence, the mouth would be last to freeze and the first to thaw. Under those conditions, icebergs could not be formed.[4]

Finally, we ask this question.

Why is it warmer the farther north you go?

As you go farther north, it at first becomes very cold. Then, as you get to the farthermost northern regions, it becomes warmer, and as Nansen found out, unbearably hot!

If it can be proved by giving examples from explorers such as Nansen (we will quote another in a moment) that as you advance to the so-called Pole it becomes warmer, that game is more plentiful than further south, then where can we say this warm climate, this heat, comes from?

It can only come from a warm northerly wind blowing from the interior of the Earth!

Reed quotes Captain C. F. Hall as follows:

We find this is a much warmer country than we expected...

We have found that the country abounds with life, and seals, game, geese, ducks, musk-cattle, rabbits, wolves, foxes, bears, partridges, lemmings, etc...[5]

Why is it that birds and some animals migrate to the far north in the winter where it is much warmer and easier for them to find food?

A. W. Greely, in his book *Three Years of Arctic Service,* wrote of birds of a species not known to us, butterflies, mosquitoes and flies![6]

Nansen was puzzled over the fox tracks that shouldn't have been there. The accepted thinking is that the farther north you go the colder it becomes, but many explorers have found quite the reverse and eventually a warm sea is reached.

This, theoretically, if the Earth is just a sphere, and not flattened at the poles, is a sheer impossibility. However, we do know that the Earth is flattened somewhat at the poles, and we have the word of numerous Arctic explorers that the weather does become warmer, that a warm sea is reached. Moreover, that animal life and game is abundant.

There can be only one answer. These animals and the warmth come from the interior of the world where there is probably a sub-tropical temperature.

15 : Secret Geodetic Surveys

Why was it that at the turn of the century, the Geodetic Survey Departments of both the French and United States governments made certain tests which upset the Copernican theory, and then decided that they should be kept secret? We feel that the results of those tests have an important relationship to the case for a hollow Earth.

The material in this chapter consists of extracts from an article written by Raymond A. Palmer (based upon one in the *Scientific American*) slightly edited by him, reproduced here with his kind permission.

If you've ever watched a bricklayer at work, you've seen him use a plumb bob to determine the perpendicular so that his wall will be erect and straight. A plumb bob is simply a weight suspended on the end of a cord. It acts on the principle of the attraction of gravity, or mass, and the weight always points towards the centre of gravity, which in the case of the spherical Earth is its exact centre.

A line formed by the cord of a plumb bob is at precisely a right angle from the horizontal. It is a division of a plane surface into two ninety-degree angles. By simply laying his bricks parallel to the line of the plumb bob, the bricklayer builds a wall that is precisely correct. If he did not use a plumb bob, there would be many more leaning Towers of Pisa in the world.

However, the plumb bob is not used only to erect buildings, but to measure the distance of the Sun or any planet.

Sometime prior to 1901, the French government, wished to determine more accurately the actual size of the Earth, so that they could revise and refine their calculations regarding the distance apart at the top of two lines perpendicular to the surface of the Earth and the bottom of those same two lines.

They wanted a pair of lines long enough to give them an

appreciable measurement. Obviously, they could not erect two parallel poles a mile high, but they did feel it was possible to suspend two plumb bobs a mile deep into a mine shaft, and thus be able to measure the distance apart at the top and the distance apart at the bottom, which would be slightly less. They wanted to know how much less.

The results of these tests were very strange. So strange that the French Geodetic scientists contacted the scientists of the American Geodetic Survey and conveyed their results to them, with the request that similar tests be conducted in the United States. Officially, nothing was done for some years.

Then, in 1901, one of the Geodetic surveyors happened to be working in the vicinity of the Tamarack mines near Calumet, Michigan. He contacted the chief engineer at Tamarack, and informed him of the information transmitted by the French government.

The mine shafts were selected, and plumb lines exactly 4,250 feet long were suspended in each mine. At the end of these lines a sixty pound bob was hung. In order to prevent movement through a horizontal direction, each bob was suspended in a tank of oil placed at the bottom of the mine shafts. In this way, it was reasoned, magnetic forces could not affect them. The lines used to suspend the bobs were No. 24 piano wires. For twenty-four hours the lines were allowed to hang, so that there would be no possibility of movement from putting them in place still remaining in the lines. The measurements were begun.

It was then that it was discovered that the French Geodetic engineers had not made a mistake. Careful re-checking proved that the lines, contrary to expectations, *were farther apart at the bottom than at the top!*

There can be only one implication from such a strange result – the centre of gravity is not, as previously believed, at the centre of the Earth, but in fact must be *above the surface of the Earth*.

Greatly puzzled, and not a little disturbed, the Tamarack engineer sent for Professor McNair of the Michigan College of Mines. With McNair there to check his results, the experiment was repeated and the measurements gone over again; both men were convinced that no error had been made.

Professor McNair suggested that the plumb bobs be changed in their substance to overcome any possibility of magnetic attraction or repulsion due to a magnetic ore body nearby. But when this was done, the same figures were arrived at. If magnetic influences had been at work, they would have varied with different metals, but they did not.

Now, suggested McNair, it would be a good idea to prevent air currents from travelling up and down the mine shafts which might be affecting the plumb lines. Thus, both mine shafts were sealed at the top. Once more the figures remained the same.

Professor McNair, when questioned, stated for publication that he had proved that magnetic attraction from the Earth or the sides of the shaft did not cause the strange divergence. Then he went back to the Michigan College of Mines and wiped the whole thing from his mind.

A second series of experiments were conducted at Calumet. This time two elevation shafts into the mine were used instead of one, those numbered two and five. These two were 4,250 feet apart, and were also 4,250 feet deep. They were connected at the bottom by a perfectly straight transverse tunnel. Now, plumb bobs were hung in each shaft, and measurements were made. This time it was found that the plumb lines were 8.22 inches farther apart at the bottom than at the top.

It did not take the Tamarack engineer long to discover that this figure exactly represents the divergence that would be necessary to complete a 360° spherical circumference. There was only one difficulty – as expressed by the plumb lines, it would be the circumference of the *inside* of a sphere, and not the outside!

Further, the centre of gravity, as expressed by the angles formed by the plumb lines, would be approximately 4,000 miles out in space!

Obviously this could not be quite true, because if the Chinese were to make calculations based on a similar pair of mine shafts, in their country on the opposite side of the globe, the centre of gravity would be found to be 4,000 miles in the *other direction*. The centre of gravity, according to the plumb lines, was a sphere's surface, some 16,000 miles in diameter. Any place, 4,000 miles up, was the centre of gravity.

Can we blame the Tamarack engineer for going down in his mine and maintaining a grim silence from that moment on?

The Earth is a sphere (with certain very minor irregularities). We live on the outside of it. The Moon circles the Earth, and the Earth circles the Sun. Some force holds them all in orbit and in their relationships to each other. It is said the Moon's orbit is maintained because the attraction of mass of both bodies is exactly counterbalanced by centrifugal force. The Earth system is maintained in its orbit about the Sun by the same delicate balance. Could it be that there is no such thing as 'attraction of mass'?

Or, could it be that the Earth is really some other shape, even hollow?[1]

Towards the end of his remarkable book, Gardner made an appeal to the government of his great country, the United States of America, to mount an expedition using both ships and aircraft for the purpose of exploring the interior of the Earth.

It would seem the U.S. government has carried out Gardner's suggestion, and that initial explorations of a few thousand miles into the interior have been made, on more than one occasion, by the U.S. Navy with aircraft under the command of that great explorer, the late Admiral Richard E. Byrd.

The Admiral made it very plain in public pronouncements that the areas visited were 'out of this world'. Those were not his words, but the descriptions he gave of the fantastic lands 'beyond the Pole' put them in that category.

Possibly Byrd made several flights some way into the interior of the earth. In recent years a 'clamp-down' seems to be operating about these flights, and the whole business is now very much 'under wraps'. This, of course, I expect to be denied. The U.S. government cannot do anything else. All the Admiral's papers are kept from public record.

According to the *Encyclopaedia Britannica*, this very distinguished American was born in 1888 and died in 1957.

The Encyclopaedia states that on 9 May, 1926, Byrd and his co-pilot, Floyd Bennett, flew over the North Pole. Then on 29 November, 1929, with three companions he flew over the South Pole. In 1947, he made a second flight over the South Pole. Finally, on 8 January, 1956, he flew over the South Pole for the third time. This great explorer and splendid man was also highly involved in organizing what became known as 'Little America' in the South Polar area, an American base there.[1]

Before commencing a flight over the South Polar area in 1947, the Admiral publicly stated:

I'd like to see that land *beyond* the Pole. That area beyond the Pole is the centre of the great unknown. (Italics mine – Author.)

Palmer wrote:

Millions of people read his statement in their daily newspapers. And millions thrilled to the Admiral's subsequent flight to the Pole and to a point 1,700 miles beyond it. Millions heard the radio broadcast description of that flight, which was also published in the newspapers...[2]

Now, here is Byrd mystery number one.

Palmer's article was referring to a flight in 1947 by the Admiral over the *North* Pole, which 'apparently' he did not make. The *Encyclopaedia Britannica* does not list a North Pole flight for 1947.

The reason for this was given in Palmer's next issue of his magazine. He knew about Byrd's flight over the South Polar area, but as a book had been published called *Worlds Beyond the Poles,* by F. Amadeo Giannini, reiterating over and over again that Byrd flew over the North Pole in 1947, and quoting complete reports from both radio and newspaper sources, Palmer decided to go on a 'fishing expedition', so to speak, to see if he could draw out something.[3]

It was just possible that the Admiral had done two polar flights that year.

Now, we present Byrd mystery number two.

Palmer lives in Amherst, Wisconsin, U.S.A. He wrote that at about three miles from him was Nelsonville, and that this was the home of Lloyd K. Grenlie, though that gentleman lived more recently in Green Bay, where he served in the Federal Aviation Agency before his death on 7 June, 1970. However, Grenlie's family are Palmer's neighbours. In Palmer's words:

This is important only because Lloyd K. Grenlie was the radio-man on Admiral Byrd's expedition to the South Pole in 1926 and to *both* poles in 1929.

It was emphatically denied that he made flights to *both* poles in 1929. That year a newsreel could be seen in America's theatres which described *both* flights, and also showed newsreel photographs of the 'land beyond the pole (north) with its mountains, trees, river, and a large animal identified as a mammoth'.

Today this newsreel apparently does not exist, although hundreds of my readers remember, as I do, this movie short. Thus, I have it on my own personal viewing of this movie short, and from the radio-man who went with Byrd to that land beyond the pole and *saw* the things recorded on that film, that this unknown, uncharted, and presently denied land exists! [4]

Palmer stated that hundreds of his magazine readers recalled seeing the newsreel. Here is a letter from one of his readers emphasizing his point.

Dear Ray Palmer,

There still seems to be considerable controversy about Admiral Byrd's flights to the North and South Poles and what he saw in the interior of the Earth at the South Pole, but nobody ever mentions the documentary film, which Byrd took on this flight in colour, and which was shown in motion picture theatres throughout the United States soon after Byrd's return home. (My sister and I saw this in White Plains, New York.)

Byrd narrated this film himself and exclaimed in wonder, as he approached a warm water lake surrounded by conifers, with a large animal moving among the trees, and what Byrd described as a 'mountain of coal, sparkling with diamonds'.

Sincerely,
Dorothy E. Graffin (Miss)[5]

Byrd and his companions should have seen nothing but ice and water. However, they were flying over a very mysterious terrain!

The Admiral's polar flights seem to be shrouded in more

than one mystery. The *Encyclopaedia Britannica* only records one polar flight by Byrd in 1929; yet the radio-man stated that there were two; one over the North Pole and one over the South Pole.

Why did Giannini in his book state that the Admiral flew over the North Pole in 1947, giving newspaper and radio sources for his information, when Byrd is on record as having only flown over the South Pole that year?

Is it possible that Byrd flew over both poles in 1929 and over both poles in 1947?

In April, 1955, the U.S. Navy announced that an expedition to the South Pole was to be led by Admiral Richard E. Byrd. It consisted of five ships, fourteen aeroplanes, special tractors and a complement of 1,393 men. The ostensible purpose was to construct a satellite base at the South Pole. This, of course, turned out to be not the real reason at all.

The following announcement is Byrd mystery number three.

In San Francisco, on the eve of his departure, Admiral Byrd delivered a radio address in which he stated: *'This is the most important expedition in the history of the world.'*

Well, no doubt it was an important expedition, but why did he claim it to be the most important in the history of the world?

On 13 January, 1956, Byrd and the U.S. Navy flew to a point 2,300 miles *beyond* the South Pole. The entire distance was stated to have been accomplished over land. *Now, if you look at your map, the South Polar continent is entirely surrounded by water!* No matter in what direction you proceed from the South Pole, hundreds of miles over water have to be traversed to reach a total distance of 2,300 miles.

It was announced by press and radio on 5 February, 1956, that: 'On 13 January, members of the United States expedition accomplished a flight of 2,700 miles from the base at McMurdo Sound, and penetrated a *land extent* of 2,300 miles *beyond the Pole.*' (Italics mine – Author.)

A point worth noting is that the International Geophysical Year research programme was planned in 1947, the year of Byrd's flight of 1,700 miles beyond the South Pole. The International Geophysical Year started in 1957, just after his flight of 2,300 miles beyond the Pole the previous year. Byrd and his expedition had by then set up 'Little America', the American base in the Antarctic. The I.G.Y. research programme involved large-scale activity in both the Arctic and Antarctic areas. Was all this just a coincidence?

An interesting point to reflect upon is that in 1929 the UFOs were not in evidence. A colour film was shown of Byrd's polar flight that year. It was in 1947, the year of Byrd's flight of 1,700 miles beyond the South Pole, that Kenneth Arnold's sighting of nine gleaming objects flying near Mt. Rainer, State of Washington, ignited the flying saucer saga in modern times. Soon after that the authorities clamped down on publicizing the Admiral's flights to the same extent.

Apropos the possibility of a 'clamp-down', Palmer published a very interesting letter in his magazine. Here is an extract from it:

Dear Mr. Palmer,

I have been told that several years ago your magazine devoted several issues to the hollow Earth theory and polar openings, and that you tried to stir up interest so people would search newspaper records concerning Byrd's expeditions to the poles...

It may interest you to know that I have uncovered so far a photo taken in 1947 by Admiral Byrd of an oasis at the Pole. The caption reads – First Picture of Mysterious Antarctic 'Oasis'. Pictured above is one of the most imagination-stimulating discoveries made by Admiral Richard E. Byrd's recent Antarctic expedition – a large ice-free area dotted with multi-colored lakes in a region hitherto considered to be perpetually blanketed by ice and snow...

If I can but recover the rest of that issue (Mr. Revis is referring to a back issue of the American *Saga* magazine – Author) it explains that Byrd found animals of prehistoric nature at the Pole and also that he thought he had crossed over to another planet. We now know that to be false but we did not see what Byrd saw. The news I speak of was suppressed or cut short immediately in 1947. That year was Byrd's second expedition to the South Pole. If these things are not, so why else are all of Byrd's papers kept from public record? Since Byrd's expeditions were government financed and controlled the answer is obvious...

Bill G. Revis.[6]

Palmer, commenting on this letter in his magazine, stated that on the Byrd flight of 1947 large animals looking like mastodons were seen, and quite rightly pointed out that the mastodon is extinct on the *surface* of this planet!

Shortly before the Admiral died in 1957, he described the newly discovered territory in these words: *'That enchanted continent in the sky, land of everlasting mystery!'*

This is the most significant and revealing of all his dramatic statements. You see, upon entering the polar opening there is an optical illusion of an 'island in the sky', this being a reflection of the Earth's surface on the sky, which has been observed by many polar explorers.

Did the Admiral fly several times some way into the interior of the Earth? I am sure that he did just that!

17: The South Polar Entrance

There have been some exceptionally well-authenticated UFO sightings in Antarctica. The first UFO sighting on record in that area occurred in March, 1950.

Commander Augusto Vars Orrego of the Chilean Navy saw a number of UFOs circling above them. The Commander's report stated:

During the bright Antarctic night, we saw flying saucers, one above the other, turning at tremendous speeds. We have photographs to prove what we saw.[1]

What happened to those photographs? As far as is known, they have never been released to the newspapers.

During January, 1956, a group of Chilean scientists had been flown by helicopter to Robertson Island in the Weddell Sea, to study the geology, fauna and other features of the locality.

Gordon Creighton described the very impressive UFO sighting these scientists experienced in an article published in *Flying Saucer Review* called 'A Cigar-Shaped UFO over Antarctica'.[2]

He wrote:

At the beginning of January, 1956, during a period of stormy weather, the party suddenly became aware of something which, in other circumstances, could have been very grave for them. This was that their radio had mysteriously ceased to function. This was however not too worrying a disaster in so much as it was firmly settled that the helicopter would return to take them off again on January 20.

At the request of the two scientists, their true names are not divulged by UFO Chile (this group sent *Flying Saucer Review* the report in their bulletin No. 2 – Author) and they are referred to herein by the substitute names of Doctor Tagle and Professor Barros...

Creighton explained that Dr. Tagle was in the habit of getting up in the night to observe anything of meteorological interest, but that the Professor, on the other hand, did not like to be disturbed. However, on 8 January, Dr. Tagle saw something so out of the ordinary that he went back to the hut and woke up the professor, who dressed and came out with him.

Dr. Tagle pointed upwards, almost overhead. Still in a bad temper through being disturbed, Barros looked as directed, and beheld two 'metallic' cigar-shaped objects in verticular positions, perfectly still and silent, and flashing vividly the reflected rays of the sun...

Soon after 7.00 a.m. they were joined by the other two members of the party, an assistant and a medical orderly. They all watched the two craft.

At about 9.00 a.m. object No. 1 (the nearest to the zenith) suddenly assumed a horizontal posture and shot away like a flash towards the west. It had now lost its metallic brightness and had taken on the whole gamut of visible colours of the spectrum, from infra-red to ultra-violet. Without slowing down it performed an incredible acute-angle change of direction, shot off across another section of the sky and then did another sharp turn as before. These vertiginous manoeuvres, the zig-zagging, abrupt stopping, instantaneous accelerating, went on for some time right overhead, the object always following tangential trajectories in respect to the Earth and all in the most absolute silence.

The demonstration lasted about five minutes. Then the object returned and took up position beside its companion in almost the same area of the sky as before, but now it was the turn of No. 2 to show its paces and do a weird zig-zagging dance. Shooting off towards the east, it performed a series of ten dispointed bursts of flight, broken by brusque changes of direction, and marked by the same colour changes when accelerating or stopping, and so on. After about three minutes of this, object No. 2 returned and took up its station near its companion, and reassumed its original solid and metallic appearance.

The scientists had with them two Geiger-Miller counters of high sensitivity, one of them auditory and the other of the flash-type. When the two objects had finished their dance and re-assumed their stations in the sky, someone discovered that the flash-type Geiger counter now showed that radioactivity around them had suddenly increased 40 times -- enough to kill any organism subjected long enough to it. The discovery greatly increased the anxiety felt by the four men, as may well be imagined ...

Although they had no telescopic lens, they did however have cameras with them, and they took numerous photographs of the objects, both in colour and black and white. We are not told in the report what became of these photographs.

While Professor Baros felt no fear that they were likely to be in danger of attack from the objects, he had to admit that with his severely rational scientific mentality he found that the idea of being confronted with such a phenomenon from beyond the realms of any known earthly science was 'anything but sooth-ing'. And as the hours passed the conviction was born in all four men that they were face to face with a phenomenon of non-human origin, that they were being spied upon by an intel-ligence that for some reason or other desired to remain anony-mous, and whose next moves were utterly unforeseeable.

The sighting of these two objects lasted altogether two days. This is a very long time for UFOs to be seen. In lighter vein, might this be suggested for inclusion in the next edition of the *Guinness Book of Records*?

To conclude Creighton's admirable report, referring to the second day:

At about 11.00 p.m. the Antarctic blizzard, a wind capable of reaching velocities of 300 km. p.h., began to get into its stride, and the sky clouded over.

At about 2.00 a.m., at the height of the storm, the scientists established that the radioactivity level had dropped. And at the same time the extraordinary psychological tensions reigning among the party had suddenly dropped too.

Even before they were able to prove it visually, the party were certain that the objects had gone.

Next day, the radioactive level was back at normal, and that evening a break in the storm brought a brief clearance of some 40 per cent of the sky, and they were able to see for themselves that the things were no longer there.

On January 20 the helicopter picked up the party. Though they did not dare report their experience officially, for fear of ridicule, they did decide to tell one man, a high-ranking officer in the Chilean Army, who heard their story calmly, without surprise. This officer knew of many sightings of UFOs, registered in almost all the expeditions to Antarctica, but he had never heard of one that lasted so long and was so precise in all its details as this. And the Air Technical Intelligence Centre (ATIC) in the U.S.A. in due course sent a lengthy questionnaire which 'Barros' and 'Tagle' completed and returned.

This sighting has everything. It starts with the radio being put out of action. This is a commonplace occurrence with UFO sightings in the near vicinity. If there had been a car, that would have been temporarily out of order These scientists saw these two objects clearly in the sky overhead absolutely crystal clear, as metallic objects. There they were in vertical positions, and they stood there like that for a very long time. Indeed, so much that Creighton in his article wrote:

They looked as if they had always been there from the beginning of time, part of the sky itself.

Then they each in turn gave magnificent displays of their capabilities as regards not only flight, but their fantastic speed, abrupt turns and sudden stops far beyond our present capabilities.

This sighting of these two cigar-shaped objects over Antarctica ranks as one of the classic ones. It is a great pity that the eyewitnesses did not allow their names to be mentioned. Nevertheless, it is an outstanding one.

Then, in July, 1965, there followed an even more authenticated sighting, though it did not last so long. This was a really first-class, multi-witness sighting. This time the witnesses included not only naval personnel from three countries, but scientists as well.

The Brazilian newspaper, *O Estado de Sao Paulo*, gave the following report with an 8 July date line:

For the first time in history, an official communiqué has been published by a government about the flying saucers. It is a document from the Argentine Navy, based on the statements of a large number of Argentine, Chilean and British sailors stationed in the naval base in Antarctica.

The communiqué declared that the personnel of Deception Island naval base saw, at nineteen hours forty minutes on 3 July, a flying object of lenticular shape, with a solid appearance and a colouring in which red and green prevailed and, for a few moments, yellow. The machine was flying in a zig-zag fashion and in a generally western direction, but it changed course several times and changed speed, having an inclination of about forty-five degrees above the horizon. The craft also remained stationary for about twenty minutes at a height of approximately 5,000 metres, producing no sound.

The communiqué states moreover that the prevailing meteorological conditions when the phenomenon was observed can be considered excellent for the region in question and the time of year. The sky was clear and quite a lot of stars were visible.

The Secretariat of the Argentine Navy also states in its communiqué that the occurrence was witnessed by scientists of the three naval bases and that the facts described by these people agree completely. It is understood that the photographs taken by a photographer at one of these bases will be made public after they have been analysed by scientists.[3]

Whatever happened to these photographs, too? There are an awful lot of excellent UFO pictures taken by the military that are being kept 'under wraps'.

There could well have been a lot of other UFO sightings in Antarctica that have not come to light. We were extremely lucky to learn of these two excellent reports, especially as in both cases military personnel were involved.

However, it would seem that the authorities in South American countries are (or should we say, were) more prone to release information about UFOs than their counterparts in Britain and the United States.

At any rate, these two sightings indicate that the UFOs are around that region. This is to be expected, for the South Polar Entrance is in Antarctica. It is not situated at the point on the map called the South Pole.

Amundsen and Scott both reached that point, the 'South Pole', and in 1956 Admiral George Dufek, of the United States Navy, landed there from the air. Since that time, a base has been established at the South Pole and has been continuously occupied by scientists doing research work.

The South Polar opening is in the region on the map of Antarctica called 'The Area of Inaccessibility'. The entrance is some distance away from the South Pole, anything from 600 to 1,800 miles. 'The Area of Inaccessibility' is quite a vast one. I you can imagine Antarctica as a clock face, then if you look at your map of the continent 'The Area of Inaccessibility' will be very roughly two o'clock from the South Pole.

It is similar in size to the hole beyond the so-called North Pole. That is, not more than 285 miles in diameter and not less than 50.

It is interesting to consider why this place is called 'The Area of Inaccessibility'. You might think that the terrain is pretty tough. That is probably true, but the real reason for its name is the result of navigation problems.

There are no bases in 'The Area of Inaccessibility', though the Russians have one on the edge. This is very significant and relates to their discoveries of 'unknown' areas at the North Pole.

In this area the magnetic compass is useless. The inertial guidance system does not function either. It is possible to reach the geographical South Pole through inertial guidance, but *not* the 'hole' in 'The Area of Inaccessibility'.

Palmer wrote:

It should be obvious why – the rotation of Earth cannot be measured accurately when you are not accurately located on the 'arc' of Earth's surface. In short, if you are not located perpendicular to any line drawn through the centre of Earth, you cannot determine the rotational speed of the planet with accuracy. In an area where the rotational speed (for example) might be 380 miles per hour, you could get a reading of zero if your angle to the perpendicular was deviated by approximately 33 degrees which you would inevitably be at a given point in your 'descent' along the slope of any depression in Earth's surface . . .

It would seem that anyone entering that area will come back out only by incredible luck.

Naturally, if we get into the area of a hollow Earth, and an inhabited one, we can conceive of some very sophisticated 'Defences' on the part of the inhabitants which might both prevent anyone from coming in, or from getting out.[4]

The polar entrances are now much more difficult to locate than before the Earth tilted on its axis thousands of years ago. In antediluvian times what are now polar areas were very likely aligned with the equator. In any case when the Flood came, the polar entrances were hidden by snow and ice.

Antarctica holds many mysteries and hidden secrets. In the last quarter of a century some remarkable discoveries have been made on that continent.

On 6 October, 1973, *The Times* published a report based on an article in an issue of *Nature* dated the previous day.

The Times stated that some seventeen 'lakes' had been found under the Antarctic ice. The discovery of the lakes had been made by Dr. G. K. A. Oswald and Dr. G. de Q. Robin, of the Scott Polar Research Institute. The newspaper reported that these lakes varied in width from 1 km to 15 km.

The lakes were located by means of a special radio-echo sounding technique. Radio pulses were sent down from the U.S. Navy plane – in which the two men were flying – and these passed through the ice and bounced off the rock below.

Some places were found where the radio-echo was much more pronounced, as if it was not being reflected off rock but from a smooth, horizontal surface. The conclusion was reached that there were lakes under the ice.

According to *Nature,* one of the lakes was discovered near Sovietskaya station during the period 1967-8; while the other sixteen were found during 1971-2 and are situated farther south.

The lake under the ice near Sovietskaya and two of the others are close to saddles on the ice surface; while the remainder are bunched together round a dome of ice which covers them to a depth of between 2.8 km and 4.2 km.

Back in February, 1947, an extremely important discovery was made of an ice-free area in the south-eastern part of Antarctica. This place is now known as Bunger's Oasis, after Lt. Commander David Bunger who found it.

At the time Bunger was piloting one of the transport seaplanes that Admiral Byrd used in Operation Highjump.

Bunger and his crew were flying inland, near the Queen Mary Coast of Wilkes Land. While only a few miles from the sea, they suddenly saw below their plane something quite different from the monotonous snow white terrain, which was their daily 'fare'.

What a shock to see ahead of them a dark brown tract of land, entirely ice-free! An area covering some three hundred square miles!

Most surprising of all were the lakes! These too were free of ice, blue- and green-coloured, and each was more than three miles in length. These lakes, according to my National Geographic Society map of Antarctica, were really inner arms of the sea, scattered among 300 square miles of bare, brown hills.

Bunger was staggered by the fact that the colours in the lake were so bright. It seemed as though something under the water caused them to reflect such vivid light.

He landed his seaplane on one of these lakes, and then

received another surprise. The water in the lake was warmer than that in the sea.

Two sides of the 'oasis' had huge, sheer walls of ice, and the others were not so steep.

There are traditions of a legendary Rainbow City in Antarctica. This may have been in the area of Bunger's Oasis. These lakes could be reflecting the colours of the city – from which its name originated – and, perhaps, Commodore Cousteau, the famous underwater explorer, should undertake an expedition to explore below their surface, and seek for the fabulous lost city.

Rainbow City was supposed to have been built thousands of years before the Flood, and all the colours of the rainbow were said to have been used in the construction of the buildings, and even in the paving of the streets.

When the earth tilted on its axis thousands of years ago, the city may have been submerged under the waters. The remains of it may be located under Bunger's Oasis, and the different colours of buildings reflecting up through the waters of the various lakes. You will recall that it seemed to Bunger as if something below the surface caused the water to give out more light than is normal.

Is Rainbow City there? A fascinating conjecture.

Further evidence that there is something very mysterious about the operation of the laws of physics in the polar areas is shown by what occurred during the launching of the first polar orbit satellites.

It is incredible that out of 17 U.S. polar experimental rocket shots, only two gave the expected result when a specific factor was introduced – a definite change in procedure which deliberately avoided a course directly over the pole.

All cones released directly over the North Pole (or from a precise polar orbit) were lost. On the other hand, all cones released over Alaska and the nearby 'polar area' were picked up.

It should be explained that when a rocket was fired into orbit over the Pole, it was calculated precisely where the nose cone would be released by a radio-triggered device. Personnel would be ready at the prescribed place to pick up or catch the nose cone as a parachute lowered it slowly to the Earth's surface.

Now, in making their calculations the technicians were presumably working on the assumption that the Earth was *completely* spherical and that there was no polar entrance to the interior.

What happened to the other 15 lost cones which did not arrive at their destinations? Was the reason that they were not picked up the fact that the nose cones were released in that mysterious area *beyond* the Pole, where the entrance to the interior of the Earth is believed by some people to be situated?

It is obvious that those early nose cones were lost because the laws of physics do not operate over the polar areas, as they do over the rest of the Earth. All these losses must have cost the American tax payers millions of dollars.

On 10 August, 1960, the Discoverer satellite was fired. The next day, after 17 passes around the Earth, the cone was released 'somewhere over the Arctic' and was retrieved from the sea north of Hawaii. On 19 August, a second cone was caught in mid-air as planned, this one having been ejected from the satellite 'over Alaska'.

Since then, a very large number of satellites have been successfully launched and some few million photographs taken in the last fourteen years for meteorological and other purposes to do with the study of man's environment.

Now, we come to what is probably the most important contribution to our case for the hollow Earth. The visual one!

In this book are reproduced the most exciting and remarkable photographs ever taken. The first one that I want to bring to your attention was taken by the ESSA-7 satellite on 23 November, 1968. This picture is of the North Pole area.

The following photograph was also taken on the same day by the same ESSA-7 satellite and this shows the South Pole area.

Both are official photographs provided by the Environmental Science Service Administration, U.S. Department of Commerce.

Both pictures show a remarkably clear photograph of the cloud cover on that day over both poles. Both depict about 40% of Earth's total area.

Up to 10 December, 1969, ESSA-7 had taken 29,953 pictures, when it was placed on standby mode. *During 481 days, the picture of the North Pole is the only one which shows a total lack of cloud cover over that area, which is otherwise perpetually and almost completely obscured by clouds.* It is this feature which is the most remarkable one concerning this photograph, although the detail and pattern of the clouds present in the picture is also remarkable.

The photograph of the South Pole is equally detailed in its cloud pattern, but unlike the North Pole picture, it shows the polar area completely covered by clouds, thus no surface detail is observable.

The North Pole photograph which does not show clouds in the polar area *reveals the surface of the planet*. Although, surrounding the polar area, and north of such regions as the North American continent, Greenland and the Asian continent, the ice fields can be observed, *we do not see any in a large circular area at the geographical pole*.

What do we see, instead? We are looking at the North Polar entrance. *The 'Hole' at the Pole!*

One of the difficulties in the past has been locating a satellite photograph that undeniably and clearly shows the polar entrance.

Now, as it happens, the North Pole 'hole' is also revealed in a photograph taken by another satellite ESSA-3, nearly two years earlier, on 6 January, 1967. On the same day ESSA-3 took a photograph of the South Polar ice cap showing cloud cover.

Out of more than a million and a half photographs showing cloud cover taken of the North Pole area up till 6 January, 1967, none of them had shown such a 'hole' before, the reason for this being the previously mentioned almost perpetual cloud cover at the Pole.

Here then, are two of the most thrilling photographs ever taken. *They are dynamite!*

Incidentally, our case is strengthened by the fact that two photographs of the hole are shown here, each taken by separate cameras in two different satellites. This will dispose of any criticism that the hole was caused by a fault in the lens of the camera.

We now present two colour photographs of Earth taken by ATS-111 satellite camera, the first one NASA 67-HC-723, taken from a height of 23,000 miles. No date was given with the colour transparency supplied by NASA.

Please note the depression at the top of the picture, something that looks like a moon crater. This could well be a picture of the entrance taken from another angle.

Now, the next picture is reproduced from the NASA book *Exploring Space with a Camera*. It is ATS-111's photograph of Earth taken on 18 November, 1967. The vantage point is the equator at approximately 47 degrees West. Once again what appears to be a moon crater can be seen at the top of the photograph.

If there are polar entrances to the interior of the Earth, this would probably be top secret classified information.

Now, these satellite photographs are in the public domain. The likelihood of anyone spotting the very few pictures showing the 'hole' would be very, very long odds indeed. Possibly, it was considered wiser to leave them available along with all the millions of others, so as not to be accused afterwards of withholding information that is in the public domain.

Palmer wrote:

If flying saucers have been in the top secret file, then the place they might come from certainly would be! Passing over the subject of flying saucers, there are many more reasons why a hole at the Pole would be classified information. Militarily, it would seem to be highly significant, particularly if the inside of the Earth is inhabited (perhaps by a race far superior to us scientifically, and technologically).[1]

The photographs taken by ESSA-3 and ESSA-7 clearly show the polar entrance. If this black area shown in the centre of the polar area is not the 'hole', then perhaps the scientists will tell us exactly what it is!

19: The Complete Case

The hollow Earth theory is only held by a small minority of people, so anyone putting forward a case for it is in a similar position to an advocate whose client has not had a good press.

Nevertheless, this 'brief' has been taken on because, sometimes, it is 'the maligned, discarded stone that is found to be the missing capstone of the Pyramid!'

Earlier, it has been emphasized how important it is to look into every facet of our subject.

The wealth of material that came to light on the hollow Earth theory was immense. The evidence has been submitted in this book. Now, it is time to present a final summary of the case.

Various points have been made that indicate the conditions are favourable for a hollow Earth.

(a) The Earth is spherical but flattened at the poles. If this was not the case, then as Reed pointed out in his own work, there would be little point in writing this book.

(b) Gardner postulated that all planets are hollow with a central sun, including the Earth. Furthermore, that everything in nature is hollow. For example, a geode stone is hollow.

(c) The old theory that the Earth had a fluid, molten core has gone into the garbage can. Modern scientific thinking has changed regarding the structure of the earth.

(d) The van Allen belts, zones of intense radiation surrounding the Earth, have gaps at each end over the polar regions. This could be a sheer coincidence, but it is very significant.

The foregoing points all indicate that the conditions are favourable for a hollow Earth.

Scientists, the military and laymen, are invited to provide alternative answers, if they can, to the following questions:

(1) Nansen, Greely and other polar explorers have found, when they got to the farthest northern regions of the polar area, the weather got warmer. What is the alternative answer to stating that this was caused by warm air blowing up through the polar entrance?

(2) Polar explorers in the far north have come across a warm sea. Why should this be?

(3) Abundant game and animal life have been discovered in these farthest north regions. Nansen was puzzled by the fox-trails. Warm-blooded animals in that area were beyond his comprehension. The only answer seems to be that they came out of the interior of the Earth.

(4) *Now here is probably one of the most important questions of all. Why did Nansen find that in the farthest north area, the north–south horizon became foreshortened while the east–west one remained constant?* Surely, this meant that he had gone over the lip of the 'hole' and was beginning to descend very gradually into the interior.

(5) If you were travelling down into the interior of the Earth, instead of proceeding horizontally on the Earth's surface, the compass needle must point up towards the North Magnetic Pole, rather than north, as it did while travelling on the surface. This is what happened in the case of Nansen. Surely, another indication that he went a little way down into the interior.

(6) Why is there so much dust in the Arctic? It has been known to float around in great clouds and fall on ships. Nansen complained bitterly about this dust. It causes the snow on which it falls to turn black. This dust has been analysed and found to be composed of carbon and iron, supposed to come out of some volcano. There are no volcanoes in the Arctic, so the only place the dust could conceivably come from is a volcano inside the Earth, blown up through the entrance.

(7) What causes coloured snow in the Arctic? This

coloured snow has also been analysed and found to contain vegetable matter, supposed to be the blossom or pollen of a plant that does not grow on the surface of the Earth. The only answer seems to be that the pollen is blown by the warm winds from the interior of the Earth.

(8) If no rivers are flowing from the inside of the Earth to the outside, then why are all icebergs composed of frozen fresh water?

Has anyone actually seen an iceberg coming out of a river? The question of icebergs has been covered earlier. The only solution appears to be that the bergs come from rivers inside the earth into that warm sea. Then, they make their way south.

(9) The two scientific committees that examined the respective claims of Peary and Cook to have reached the North Pole were extremely dubious as to whether either of them got there. It is part of our case that there is no such thing as a North Pole point. If the Earth was completely spherical with no polar entrance to the interior, that would put quite a different complexion on the whole business.

(10) Those airliners advertised as flying over the North Pole do nothing of the kind. Magnetic compasses and gyro compasses are virtually useless over a very wide area of the Arctic.

No commercial airline could afford to allow aircraft to get lost and endanger the lives of the passengers.

(11) The Russian discoveries in the polar area have been discussed. They have found that the Pole, magnetically speaking, is not just a point, but extends for at least 1,500 miles across the polar basin in the Arctic area.

Furthermore, let us reflect upon the tremendous implications of the quotation from the Russian data:

Exploration and research have shown that an enormous region of the Earth's surface and *correspondingly large realms of the unknown* may be brought within the compass of human understanding in a very few years. (Italics mine – Author)

That sentence is packed with dynamite! It would seem the Russians have, indeed, let the 'cat out of the bag'.

Apropos these Russian discoveries, I spoke recently to Ray Palmer over the transatlantic telephone, and he said that intelligence officers from SAC (Strategic Air Command) had been trying to stop him writing about the 'hole at the Pole' in his magazine. Subsequently, a letter came from Palmer confirming this had occurred.

Since then, a further issue of *Flying Saucers* has arrived. In this editorial Palmer wrote:

So our research into the possibility of a hole at the Pole is a ridiculous fantasy? Then why is the Air Force's SAC spending so much time (including 1½-hour phone call) to get us to drop the subject? SAC, they say, flies a 'grid' in the Pole area which covers the entire top of the world, and every day at least one SAC atom bomber flies directly over that spot we say has a hole! And they see no hole. But they will not provide even one plane's 'flight plan' with its navigation computations, so that we can demonstrate where it cannot possibly approach within 640 miles of the geographic pole. The Russians published their findings that the Magnetic Pole is not a point at all, but a line 1,500 miles long – as revealed in *Scientific American*. The so-called newly discovered mountain range called the Lomonsov Ridge, strangely enough, is as long as the Magnetic Pole, and exists in exactly the same location! The 'ridge' was discovered through ocean soundings, mostly from space satellites, but also by submarine and ship and aircraft radar. Computations of photos taken from space showing the hole (we've published three of them) also, strangely enough, give a 'circumference' of the rim of the hole which measures 1,500 miles. All three coincide! The water can be shallow on the 'ridge' because of centrifugal force! And obviously, any SAC 'grid' flown by stellar navigational observations, based on a 'curvature' of the Earth, as a sphere 8,000 miles in diameter, will be in serious error when taken from an area where the curvature is significantly more pronounced. The 'grid' becomes a diamond-shaped 'web' that describes a *circle*, not a partial hemisphere.[1]

(12) Consider those secret geodetic surveys by the French

and American governments, resulting in a complete upset in established scientific thought, in that the centre of gravity is not inside the Earth, but any point 4,000 miles out in space! Surely, this indicates that the shape of the Earth is not what it has been thought to be. It may even be hollow.

(13) The polar flights of the late Admiral Richard E. Byrd are full of mystery.

Why did the Admiral state publicly before the start of his 1947 flight over the South Polar area, 'I'd like to see that land *beyond* the Pole. That area *beyond* the Pole is the centre of the great unknown.'? (Italics mine – Author)

Why did he say on another occasion in a radio broadcast before leaving the U.S.A. for Antarctica, 'This is the most important expedition in the history of the world'?

Perhaps the most significant comment the Admiral made was just before his death in 1957, when he referred to the newly discovered land as 'that *enchanted continent in the sky*, land of everlasting mystery!' (Italics mine – Author)

Mention has been made earlier that some of the polar explorers who, unknowingly, have gone a little way into the interior have noticed the optical illusion of an 'island in the sky'.

This surely is an indication that the Admiral did fly some way into the interior of the Earth.

(14) Finally, the satellite photographs in this book have provided visual evidence of the North Polar entrance. Most of the year there is continuous cloud cover and fog over the area where the North Polar entrance is located.

Two photographs of the North Polar region, without cloud cover, taken by the cameras of two different satellites, are included in this book. Both clearly indicate the surface of the Arctic continent and the black circular spot which is the polar entrance to the interior of the Earth. It would be interesting to know what else this dark area could be.

THE CASE RESTS.

Part Three   The Case for Inner Earth People

If various races live inside the Earth, it would be only reasonable that they surfaced occasionally, even at times by accident. One of the most remarkable cases on record happened in England and concerns the Green Children of Wolfpittes. This is of especial interest, if we bear in mind the references in the first part of this book by both Peter Kolosimo and Harold T. Wilkins, to an underground source of energy giving out a green fluorescence.

Wilkins relates this story in another of his books, *Flying Saucers Uncensored.*[1]

The twelfth-century monk, Gervase of Tilbury, tells of 'The Green Children', who emerged from some caves or pits, in Suffolk, in such queer circumstances that one might conclude either that they had been teleported from some world in space, or from some terrestrial subterranean world! This story is also given by three other monastic chroniclers: William of Newburgh, Walsingham, and Giraldus Cambrensis.

Gervase titled it: 'De Viridibes Pueris':

'There is a village in England, some four to five miles from the noble monastery of the blessed king and martyr, Edmund, near which may be seen certain strange and memorable antiquities, called in the English "Wolfpittes". (N.B. The modern Woolpit, seven miles from Bury St. Edmunds, Suffolk.) They give their name to the adjacent village. There came a harvesttide when the reapers were gathering in the corn. On a sudden, there crept out from these two pits a boy and a girl, green at every point of their body, and clad in garments of strange colour and unknown texture. They wandered distraught about the field, until the harvesters took pity on them and brought them to the village, where many thronged to see them, marvelling at the strangeness of the occurrence. And for some days these children refused all food that was placed before them. But it happened that some beans were brought in from the fields, and the two children snatched at them greedily and sat in the pits, weeping bitterly; for they found the pods empty. Then one of the bystanders offered them only shelled beans, which they took gladly and ate forthwith. On this food they were nourished for some days, until they learnt to eat bread. At length, under the prevailing influence of our food, they slowly changed the colour of their skin, and learned to speak English. Then, on the advice of wise folk, they received holy baptism; but the boy, who seemed the junior in age, lived for only a brief time thereafter, while his sister throve and lived on, differing in no wise from the girls of our own country. The story goeth that she later married a man at Lynn (King's Lynn, Norfolk?) where she is still said to be living, or was so said, up to a few years ago.

'These two strange children were often asked whence they came, and replied: "We are folk of St. Martin's Land; for he is the chief saint among us. We know not where the land is, and remember only that one day we were feeding our father's flock in the field, when we heard a great noise like bells, as when at St. Edmund's they all peal together, and suddenly we were rapt up in the spirit and found ourselves in your harvest-field. Among us no sun riseth, nor is there open sunshine, but such a twilight as here goes before the rising and setting of the sun. Yet a land of light is to be seen not far from us, but severed from us by a stream of great breadth." '

That concludes Gervase of Tilbury's account of the Green Children, reproduced from Wilkins's book. The remarks in brackets in the story were made by Mr. Wilkins. Incidentally, Gervase of Tilbury lived around the late 12th and early 13th centuries.

Wilkins commented on Gervase's account, as follows:

It is difficult, at this stretch of time, to estimate on what basis of fact this story may rest. Obviously, a certain amount of Catholic hagiology has been imported into it ...

Then, in a footnote, Wilkins wrote:

'St. Martin's Land' is probably Merlin's land of 'Grammarye', or necromancy: a subterranean world, or twilight land, to which the 'gods', or god-men, were forced to descend after the submersion of Greater Atlantis. Hints of it are found in Amero-Indian myths and folk-lore, from Patagonia to Alaska; and there are obscure references to it in the tradition told to Egede, the missionary, by Greenlanders who said that the first Greenlander came out of a subterranean world. The American soldier, John Cleve Symmes, actually petitioned both houses of a derisive Congress to grant him a ship, in 1823, to find the North Polar opening to an inner sphere, or underground world 'which was warm and fertile, and well stocked with fruits and vegetables'.

Before merely dismissing Symmes as 'a madman', as did le Comte de Volney of the Académie des Sciences, at Paris, in 1822, let it be recalled that no one has cleared up the mystery of the 'marked reindeer', with clipped ears, shot in desolate Spitzbergen in 1876. The first statement on this point was made in 1705 by Nicolaus Witsen, a Dutchman, in his 'Noort ooster gedeelte van Asia en Europa'. He says that reindeer, far remote from any living man in the Arctic, are found mysteriously marked in the ears and on the horns, and that he himself heard hunters, in Norway, who were well acquainted with the care of reindeer, state positively that, in and before A.D. 1700, they had shot reindeer in Spitzbergen – totally uninhabited – clipped in the ears. These Spitzbergen reindeer are smaller and plumper than other Arctic breeds.

One would like also to know more about these 'Wolf-pittes' at Woolpit, Suffolk, and whether there exist deep caves or subterraneans in this part of Suffolk.

21: Deros and Teros

A book about a possible hollow Earth and its inhabitants cannot be written without some space being given to the claims of Richard S. Shaver.

On 21 May, 1951, *Life* magazine printed eight pages of material on the Shaver Story. The reader response was overwhelming and the feature created more interest than any other articles *Life* had published up to that time.

The Shaver stories were originally published by Ray Palmer in *Amazing Stories* magazine in 1944 and the series ran for four years. Thousands of readers wrote in asserting that they were true, regardless of the fact that Palmer had published them as science fiction.

Shaver maintains that the stories are factual, and claims to have been inside the interior of the Earth.

Palmer, reporting on the Shaver story, wrote:

Briefly what Mr. Shaver says is this: 'The Earth is inhabited underground, in gigantic caves whose area is a great deal more than the surface land area, by a race of people called by him "abandonero", or descendents of an abandoned group of people who were unable to leave the planet some 12,000 (or more) years ago in a general exodus made necessary by the discovery that the sun had commenced to hurl death-dealing radiations over the entire planet ...'

Shaver states that there are two groups of people in the caves. He terms them the 'dero' and the 'tero'. The dero have degenerated into midget-like idiots. On the other hand, the tero have managed to maintain a higher mental state.

Palmer added:

However, down the centuries the dero have become more

numerous and the tero reduced by constant attack to a few scattered groups in hiding who are unable to circumvent the devilry of the dero. The dero have access to the wonderful machines of the ancients, still in working order, since they were built almost indestructible, and with these machines they are able to bedevil both the tero and surface people. Among these machines are marvellous vision rays that can penetrate miles of solid rock picking up scenes all over the Earth without the need of a broadcast unit; transportation by teleportation instantaneously from one point to another (although this did require a sending and receiving set); mental machines which caused seemingly solid illusions, dreams, hypnotic compulsions (which account for the strange 'urges to kill' of surface folk, such as the case of the young girl who said 'God told me to stab mother with a knife').

They have death rays, space ships, giant rockets that traverse the upper air (the flying saucers were described in detail by Mr. Shaver before they actually appeared to Mr. Kenneth Arnold and to thousands since), ground vehicles of tremendous power, machines of the revitalizing of sex known as 'stim' machines (in which these degenerates sometimes spend their whole lives in a sexual debauch that actually deforms their bodies in horrible ways almost beyond mentioning), ben rays which heal and restore the body, but are also capable of restoring lost energy after a debauch, and many more marvellous things which Mr. Shaver claims would revolutionize our surface science if we could but obtain them . . .

'Today,' says Mr. Shaver, 'the deros still exist in the caves and all our troubles are caused by them. Our wars are fostered by them; our terrible air accidents are not always accidents at all, but the result of destructive rays aimed at them by idiots whose only delight is death and torture; even our nightmares are the result of their "dream mech" trained on us in our sleep . . .'[1]

That is a very brief résumé of the Shaver saga. Thousands of people have written to both *Life* magazine and to Ray Palmer, the original publisher, confirming that the stories are true.

Over a century ago, the famous French novelist, Jules

Verne, wrote a most exciting book called *Journey to the Centre of the Earth.* This was originally published in France during 1864.[2]

Jules Verne was a very imaginative story teller, and could be called one of the first science fiction writers. He wrote many other successful books in that vein but this particular one had a tremendous vogue. It caught the imagination of the public in a big way; just as Tolkien's books were to do in this day and age.

The book is absolutely fascinating in the light of what has been discussed in these pages. It has often been said that science fiction writers have an uncanny habit of describing inventions and events in their books which actually come about sooner or later. This is very true.

Verne's story was really fantastic. It was about a scientist who found an opening leading down into the centre of the earth. A whole group of people, including a Nordic farmer with his goose called Gertrude, make their way down through wonderful caverns covered in radiant crystals.

A most remarkable book was written some years ago called *The Smoky God*, by Willis George Emerson.[3] It describes the amazing experiences of a Norwegian, Olaf Jansen.

Mr. Emerson became friendly with the old Norseman in Southern California just prior to the latter's death. The old man gave Emerson some maps and papers, and told him a fantastic story.

Jansen and his father were fishermen. On one of their trips they sailed farther north than ever before, and eventually found themselves inside the Earth. They met up with some friendly giants who extended hospitality to them. Jansen and his father were shown many marvellous things.

Eventually, they sailed on a river right through the interior of the Earth and emerged somewhere in Antarctica. Unfortunately, shortly afterwards, their boat hit an iceberg. Jansen's father was drowned and their ship lost. Jansen, clinging precariously to the iceberg, was picked up by a Scottish whaler. When he told his tale to the captain, the poor chap was put in irons and regarded as mentally deranged. The ship duly docked at Stockholm, and Jansen was committed to a mental asylum, where he spent the next 28 years of his life.

The book is named after the dull-red sun surrounded by white vapour inside the Earth. This is interesting, as Marshall B. Gardner postulated that all planets are hollow and have central suns.

Whether you believe Olaf Jansen's story or not, it is a splendidly exciting one. Emerson wrote the tale as fiction because it was difficult to put over as fact.

It is possible that some long forgotten memory of the inner Earth still persists in the subconscious minds of people today. Consider the tremendous impact of the late Professor J. R. R. Tolkien's book, *The Lord of the Rings*, about Middle Earth.[4] He was a wonderful writer and told a spellbinding tale. His stories remind us of the old Arthurian tales in one sense. The main theme of Tolkien's stories is the constant duel between the forces of good and evil. Shaver, in his tales of Deros and Teros, is really discussing the same eternal theme.

The Tolkien books have probably sold millions of copies. Indeed, a whole cult has grown up around them. Professor Tolkien discounted any idea of their having any basis in fact, and stated that they were just stories. Nevertheless, their impact on readers has been traumatic.

This all ties in to some considerable extent with all the people who wrote to *Life* magazine and Ray Palmer about the Shaver stories. It seems that there is something buried in the subconscious mind of humanity that reacts to both Shaver's claims and to Tolkien's magnificent stories.

22 : Are we being put off the Track?

Over the last few years many ufologists, including myself, had come round to the view that most of the UFO activity emanated from an invisible area interpenetrating our planet, rather than from the old widely accepted extra-terrestrial point of origin. This viewpoint came about to some extent through the ability of both the UFOs and the ufonauts to materialize and dematerialize, and perform many other feats, pointing to the probability that they emerged into our plane of existence from another order of matter. That is, from an invisible realm.

In my last book, *The Eternal Subject*, there was a section devoted to showing a possible connection between UFOs and psychic phenomena. It is more than possible that UFO entities manipulate a good deal of psychic phenomena.[1]

Many ufologists consider that the ufonauts pretend to come from Mars, Venus, Jupiter and all stop-over points out in space, so as to confuse us and not disclose their real place of residence.

It is just possible that they materialize and dematerialize, teleport people and bring out poltergeist activity for the same reason. In short, to confuse us still further and put into our minds the idea of an invisible realm as their habitat. After all, Mr. Shaver may be right. He has told us that the dero can do all these amazing feats. Once again, perhaps we are being put off the track.

The answer may lie literally beneath our feet! If a race of people are living in the interior of the Earth, then they would have been resident there for at least 12,000 years. Furthermore, if it is true that inner Earth people have the use of wonderful machines, flying saucers and the old Atlantean 'magical' powers, then they may well possess extrasensory abilities and be able to manipulate psychic phenomena, besides performing all the wonders mentioned earlier.

The well-known American writer on UFOs, John A. Keel, discussing non-psychic UFO phenomena in an article published in *Saga* magazine, wrote:

There is, however, a mountain of evidence indicating that the force behind the UFO phenomenon is solidly based on this planet. And it has been conning us for years to keep us from discovering this fact.[2]

It should be made clear that Keel was not advocating a hollow Earth in his article but pointing to our planet as a base for UFOs. However, he is getting warm! It is more than possible that they do have a base on the surface but that is not their point of origin.

The ufonauts have been leading us a pretty dance for a very long time. According to Keel, they have been dropping artifacts all over the place for years. *However, the important point is that what they have deposited on our soil are very earthly substances, such as aluminium, silicon, magnesium and calcium.* These particularly earthly substances, as Keel has pointed out, are ignored by most ufologists looking for artifacts of an 'out of this world' nature.

Keel put it in these words:

A far more bitter truth is the sobering fact that the UFO enthusiasts and their organizations have overlooked a mountain of evidence themselves, often suppressing such evidence because it doesn't conform with their dogged belief in extraterrestrial visitations. If they systematically collected all the physical materials dropped from flying saucers in the past 25 years they would now have their own warehouse full of proof.

Keel cited many examples of earthly substances being dropped by UFOs, and for this reason the U.S. Air Force wrote many alleged landings off as hoaxes. In his article Keel mentioned a landing at Glassboro, New Jersey, back in 1964. Apparently, a small amount of potassium nitrate was found at the site, so the Air Force considered the whole affair a human hoax, even though there were markings on the ground, identical with those at other landing sites.

Keel quoted case after case of UFOs landing and dropping earthly substances, chiefly in the form of chemicals.

For example:

Thousands of miles away, on 27 October, 1954, a formation of glowing objects appeared over a crowded football stadium in Florence, Italy. A shower of shining flakes fell on the crowd from the sky. When these were analysed by the Chemical Institute of the University of Milan they were found to be composed of magnesium, iron, silicon, and calcium.

Silicon is one of the most common substances. Silica is ordinary sand. Heat it and then cool it and you have glass. Silicon can be made into all kinds of plastic objects. An almost endless variety of silicic objects and substances have been found at UFO landing sites during the past 25 years. It most often appears as a purplish liquid which resembles ordinary fuel oil. Indeed, it is sometimes mistaken for oil. When a fertilizer salesman named Reinhold Schmidt reported seeing a UFO land near Kearney, Nebraska, in 1957, investigating police officers found a puddle of this fluid at the site and accused Schmidt of putting it there himself.

Another outstanding case took place on 19 August, 1965, on a farm outside Cherry Creek, N.Y. Harold Butcher, 16, was milking cows at 8.20 p.m. when the portable radio in the barn was suddenly drowned out by static and the tractor running the milking machine abruptly stopped. Outside, a Holstein bull chained to a steel bar by a ring through its nose began to bellow. Young Butcher ran to the window and looked out. He saw a large egg-shaped object trailing a reddish vapour and emitting a steady beep-beep sound as it touched down in a nearby field. A few moments later it flew away, Butcher said, leaving behind a strange smell and several globs of a shimmering purplish liquid.

The Kawecki Chemical Company later performed a chemical analysis and found that the liquid was composed of silicon, aluminium and iron.

I could give you many, many more examples from Keel's

informative article, but there is a saying, 'enough is as good as a feast'.

Subsequently, Keel went on to state:

Unfortunately, after all these years of research, study and investigation by thousands of people and scores of scientists operating outside the Air Force and government, there is still no evidence to back up the notion that flying saucers come from outer space. There is, on the other hand, considerable evidence that real UFOs are of earthly manufacture and are piloted by normal human beings (excluding those landings and contacts which seem more in the nature of psychic phenomena). What's more, there is evidence that persons who dress and look like us (and probably are earthlings) are often engaged in collecting UFO artifacts, arriving on the scene before the original witnesses have had a chance to tell anyone about what they have just seen.

Very often, Keel stated, these foreign-looking men search the site. He quoted many modern examples of this strange activity but also gave an example from shortly after the turn of the century. This incident was reported in the London *Daily Mail*, of 20 May, 1909, and the news story told of a clerk who had seen five 'foreigners' at a landing site in Wales, taking measurements and photographs.

Who are these mysterious foreign-looking men that turn up so quickly on these occasions? Obviously, not CIA agents. That agency was not formed until after the attack on Pearl Harbour in the last world war. Mention is made of the CIA because they have been accused of being involved with the UFO situation on many occasions. No doubt, they are involved to some extent, but only if physical objects invading American air space become a national security problem. I suggest that these foreign-looking men are much more likely to be very closely associated with the ufonauts. We will be going into this interesting aspect of the problem later on.

Now, let us pause for a moment, and consider what all the foregoing means.

If, as Keel says, the UFOs are piloted by earthlings, then those craft could not have been manufactured on the Earth's surface by any country. You just couldn't keep flying 'top secret' flying saucers all over the world for over 25 years without someone 'spilling the beans'!

The fact that the ufonauts look like ourselves and have been dropping *earthly* substances indicates that they come from the Earth. However, if these craft are not manufactured *on* the surface, then they must come from *within* the Earth. It is as simple as that.

The quotations from John A. Keel's article 'The UFO Evidence Everyone Ignores' are from *Saga* Magazine, copyright © 1973 by Gambi Publications.

23 : They Knew Too Much

One of the stranger aspects of the flying saucer phenomena is the 'silencing' of well-known ufologists by the mysterious 'Men in Black'.

The first known 'Man in Black' case in modern times was the Maury Island affair in 1947. The late Edward J. Ruppelt, former head of the United States Air Force Project Blue Book, stated in his book, *The Report on Unidentified Flying Objects*, that the two principals in the case, Harold A. Dahl and Fred L. Crisman, had confessed to perpetrating a hoax. The result was that the Air Force took no further interest in the matter.[1]

The only people hoaxed were the Air Force, including two military intelligence officers who lost their lives on their way back from Tacoma to California.

Let us recapitulate what happened at lonely Maury Island on 21 June, 1947, three days before Kenneth Arnold's sighting which triggered off press publicity in a big way for flying saucers.

Harold A. Dahl, a harbour patrolman, was out in his boat on the east bay of Maury Island, near Tacoma, State of Washington, with a crew of two men and his son. Dahl's dog was also in the boat.

Suddenly Dahl, who was at the wheel, noticed:

... six very large doughnut-shaped aircraft. I would judge they were at about 2,000 feet above water and almost directly overhead. At first glance I thought them to be balloons as they seemed to be stationary. However, upon further observation, five of these strange aircraft were circling very slowly around the sixth one which was stationary in the centre of the formation. It appeared to me that the centre aircraft was in some kind of trouble as it was losing altitude fairly rapidly. The other aircraft stayed at a distance of about two hundred feet above the centre one as if they were following the centre one down. The centre aircraft came to rest almost directly over-head at about five hundred feet above the water.

All on board our boat were watching these aircraft with a great deal of interest as they apparently had no motors, propellers, or any visible signs of propulsion, and to the best of our hearing they made no sound. In describing the aircraft I would say they were at least one hundred feet in diameter. Each had a hole in the centre, approximately twenty-five feet in diameter. They were all a sort of shell-like gold and silver colour. Their surface seemed of metal and appeared to be burled, because when the light shone on them through the clouds they were brilliant, not all one brilliance, but many brilliances, something like a Buick dashboard . . .[2]

Dahl had managed to manoeuvre his boat close in to the shore. He was able to take some photographs of the objects. Suddenly, there was a dull boom and the centre object disgorged a large quantity of white, light metal pieces. This was followed by what seemed to Dahl and his companions a hail of blacker metal, which had a similar appearance to lava rock. Dahl's son had his arm injured by one of the falling fragments and another piece killed his dog. The pieces appeared to be hot for when they hit the bay steam rose from the water.

When this extraordinary deluge of metal ceased, all six of the 'aircraft' rose and drifted out to sea. The centre object, which had dropped the metal, did not seem in any way disturbed and remained in the centre as the group moved away.

Dahl stated that his boat had been damaged by the falling fragments. The crew managed to return in it to Tacoma, where Dahl reported the incident to Fred L. Crisman, his immediate chief. The latter thought Dahl and the others had been on a drinking spree. He did not, at first, believe their story. However, Dahl gave Crisman his camera with its load of film, and some of the pieces of metal, as proof. According to Dahl:

The film from our camera, developed, showed these strange aircraft, but the negatives were covered with spots similar to a negative that has been close to an X-Ray room before it has been exposed, except that the spots printed white instead of black as is the usual case.

Early in the next morning something strange happened to Dahl. One of those rather frightening things that seem to come the way of people who know too much about certain aspects of flying saucers.

A man, dressed in black, called at his home and invited him out to breakfast. Dahl was used to lumber buyers calling on him early and at first thought there was nothing unusual about his visitor. *That is until, over the breakfast table, the man described in full detail everything that had occurred to Dahl and his crew the day before.* It was quite uncanny. The man in black told Dahl that if he valued his own welfare and that of his family he should not discuss his experiences with anyone.

Early that morning, too, Crisman went over to Maury Island and found all the debris, exactly as Dahl had reported. Then, according to Crisman:

> While I stood looking at the fragments, holding a few pieces in my hand, one of the same kind of aircraft that Harold described to me came right out of a large fat cumulus cloud and made a wide circle of the little bay.

All these events were related to Kenneth Arnold, the man who saw nine gleaming objects flying near Mt. Rainier, State of Washington, three days after Dahl's encounter with six doughnut-shaped ones at Maury Island. Arnold had flown to Tacoma to investigate the affair at the request of Ray Palmer. He sent for Captain E. J. Smith, a United Airlines pilot, to come and join him. Captain Smith had also seen a gaggle of saucers from his airliner soon after Arnold's own sighting. The two pilots continued the investigation together from the Winthrop Hotel in Tacoma. After a while, they decided to bring in two intelligence officers from Hamilton Air Force Base, Captain William Davidson and Lieutenant Frank Brown. Both Arnold and Smith had been interrogated by these officers after their own sightings, and had a regard for their capabilities.

Dahl and Crisman were both agreeable to this step, but the strange affair took on a new slant when the intelligence officers arrived at the Winthrop Hotel. Dahl and Crisman gave the impression of making the whole business appear a hoax. Davidson and Brown suddenly threw in their hands, and decided to fly back to California in their B-25 bomber.

Just before the two officers left, Crisman drove up in a great hurry with a load of fragments. These were transferred to the intelligence officers' vehicle, and went with them to be eventually loaded on to the bomber. Half an hour after takeoff, the B-25 crashed near Kelso, Washington. Davidson and Brown were both killed.

Subsequently, another intelligence officer, a Major Sanders, interviewed both Arnold and Smith in Tacoma. Later, he took them both in his car to the beach at Maury Island, and pronounced the fragments alleged to have fallen there as nothing but ordinary slag. Nevertheless, he made sure of taking away with him all the pieces that Arnold had at the hotel for analysis.

Those are the main facts of this fantastic case. Let us look at one or two points. First Dahl's description of the objects as 'aircraft'. This should be borne in mind and is a factor in Dahl's favour. The second point is that he described the objects as doughnut-shaped. Now, this is very important and it is on this description that possibly the whole matter hinges!

Neither Arnold nor Smith described their objects as doughnut-shaped. They were discs, though I understand that Arnold's were more crescent-shaped. Since 1947, the bulk of the sightings have been disc- or saucer-shaped objects, although there have been plenty of other shapes thrown in for good measure – triangular, star, oval, tadpole, delta and cigar-shaped, among others. Doughnut-shaped objects have been rare, but they have been seen and photographed.

The point is that from Arnold's sighting onward – for a very long time – those who reported seeing what are termed 'flying saucers' did not report doughnut-shaped ones. Therefore, if Dahl and Crisman were concocting a hoax (quite apart from subsequently making it appear to be one), why did they pick on doughnuts? If you or I were going to perpetrate a flying saucer hoax at that time (and the time is so important) would we pick on such a shape? It is to be doubted.

Furthermore, if you or I did by such long odds pick on doughnuts for our hoax on 21 June, 1947, we would think it incredible that a doughnut-shaped UFO was photographed over New York City almost eight years later, *and was identical in size and characteristics.*

On Sunday, 15 May, 1955, Warren Siegmond saw for a period of about one minute and a half an unidentified flying object over Union Square, New York City. This important sighting was fully described in *Flying Saucer Review.*[3]

It was a beautiful day, and so, quite naturally, Mr. Siegmond was taking some pictures, on the roof of the office building, with a small reflex-type camera of Miss Jeannine Bouillier, who worked for the French Government Tourist Office.

Suddenly, Miss Bouillier pointed up at the sky behind her friend, exclaiming, 'Quick, take a look at that!'

Mr. Siegmond turned and looked in the direction she had indicated. He saw an enormous circular object, radiating like an immense ball of fire. Siegmond said he had never seen anything like it before in his life. It was a tremendous size. He started taking pictures. The object had no wings, no tail and no markings. It made no sound.

'... It didn't seem to know what gravity was. If it did know it certainly wasn't respecting it...' Siegmond declared. He managed to get several photographs of the object, one of which clearly showed its doughnut shape.

The *World Telegram* broke the news of this sighting with a big front page story. The Telephoto Service of the United Press sent the photographs to every part of the world. Mr. Siegmond showed the pictures to the United States Air Force Office of Special Investigations. They examined the negatives and agreed that he had seen something.

Another extremely well-authenticated sighting of a doughnut-shaped object occurred on 21 September, 1961. Two Boeing 707s encountered a large UFO over the Pacific. One was a B.O.A.C. aircraft, with Captain R. F. Griffin in command, and the other was a Pan American airliner. Both captains radioed to FAA towers at Wake Island and Honolulu reports on the enormous object they had seen.

Captain Griffin's B.O.A.C. airliner was flying at 37,000 feet, when the UFO showed up. 'Suddenly, we saw this bright ring in the sky, about 50 degrees up.' He described the object as round, with clearly defined edges, and pointed out that it had '*a very clear hole*' in the centre.

The Pan American skipper confirmed Captain Griffin's report. Captain Griffin added that the UFO was travelling in their direction but at a much greater speed and that it went over the horizon in seven minutes. The object must have been enormous to have been seen in such detail at such an altitude!

Surely, these two remarkable sightings of doughnut-shaped UFOs over New York in 1955 and over the Pacific in 1961 go a long way to establishing that the Maury Island affair was no hoax.

The all-important question is repeated; if Dahl was carrying out a hoax, is it likely that he would have picked on doughnut-shaped saucers at that time? Remember flying saucers were only just beginning to get publicity and no doughnut ones had been seen prior to Dahl's sighting.

Incidentally, another point that may not have impressed the intelligence officers was the dropping of slag from the centre craft. This may have stretched their credulity overmuch. *In 1947 it was not known that the UFOs are in the habit of dropping earthly substances on the surface of our planet.* Times have changed. This is something that has been learnt over the years.

The fact that slag was alleged to have been dropped from the centre UFO was probably an insult to the intelligence of the two officers. In 1947, if you were going to perpetrate a hoax connected with flying saucers, slag would have been the last thing to include in your plans. Therefore, the dropping of the slag, in the light of what is known now, is another very important factor in favour of Dahl and Crisman. The Maury Island affair was no hoax!

The intriguing question as to why Dahl and Crisman, when confronted with Davidson and Brown, appeared to make the whole affair at Maury Island out to be a hoax is, indeed, quite another matter. *Maybe the gentleman in a black suit who invited Dahl out to breakfast can answer that one.*

Can we assume for a moment that a hollow Earth exists and that people do live inside it? If we can do just that, a lot of very important events that have occurred in the past 25 years or more fit into place.

Veteran ufologists will recall the sensational closing down of Albert K. Bender's International Flying Saucer Bureau back in 1953.

At that time, Bender had quite a large international movement. He had been in close touch with Edgar Jarrold, another ufologist, who headed the Australian Flying Saucer Bureau, and they had been working together on a theory linking the UFOs with Antarctica.

Mr. Bender had written an article for publication in his magazine which divulged the secret of the saucers. That article was never published. Three 'Men in Black' visited Bender at his home. They so frightened Bender that for a long time he gave up all UFO research. This incident has been fully described by Gray Barker in his book, *They Knew Too Much About Flying Saucers.*[4]

Bender's colleagues questioned him afterwards for some time and with his permission tape-recorded his answers. One of the questions put to him was: 'How did you find out about it? Can't you tell me just where you got your theory.'

Bender's answer was, 'All I can say is this: It was something that I was thinking about for a long time, I went into the fantastic and came up with the answer.'

Now, that answer is very significant. An extra-terrestrial origin for the saucers would not be in the 'Fantastic' for a UFO researcher. What would be in the realm of the fantastic would be an inner Earth concept. If it is also noted that both Bender and Jarrold were working on a theory to do with Antarctica, you will get my message.

If it can be tentatively accepted that such an inner world exists (and proof has been presented in the second part of this book), and that the occupants have the use of fantastic machines, as well as extra-sensory powers, then it is too easy for them to frighten people into silence. If they look like us to a great extent, then they probably have their representatives here on the surface who may be the 'Men in Black'. Living just below us inside the Earth, with all their wonderful machines and advanced knowledge, it would be only too easy for them to monitor our languages, and they probably know more about us than we do ourselves.

Therefore, as I have just written, it would be easy to frighten people into silence, if they wanted to do so. After all, ufologists have wives and families, and how many police officers are going to believe statements that UFO researchers are being threatened by denizens of the inner world! In any case, the police have a full time job coping with crimes committed by members of another underworld.

Consider the case of the late Dr. Morris K. Jessup, a professional astronomer. He was, also, a prominent ufologist and wrote several fine books on the subject. Jessup believed that the majority of the UFOs emanated from what he called the binary Earth–Moon system. He considered the UFOs came from installations inside the interior of the Moon and from inside the Earth, and that they had bases in the oceans too. I think that this latter point is also very valid. In the Introduction to this book I referred to the work by the late Ivan T. Sanderson called *Invisible Residents*. He produced a mass of evidence pointing to the fact that many of the UFOs had been seen to dive in and out of the oceans, and postulated that they probably had bases there. As I write these words, I am thinking of several American newspaper cuttings that have landed up on my desk from correspondents in the United States in the last few days. One of those periodical UFO 'flaps' is in progress, but several of the news stories relate to something that would have been right up Sanderson's 'street' if he had been still with us today. We sorely miss him, a very fine man. Here is the account straight from the *Boston Herald American*, dated Saturday, 13 October, 1973:

THERE WERE THESE STRANGE CREATURES...

Pascagoula, Miss. (UP) – Two shipyard workers who claimed they were hauled aboard a UFO and examined by silvery-skinned creatures with big eyes and pointed ears were checked at a military hospital yesterday and found to be clear of radiation.

Air Force doctors at nearby Keesler Air Force Base examined the men, Charles Hickson, 42, and Calvin Parker, 19, as a precautionary measure after they came forth with their weird tale.

Officials said the men, both employed at Walker Shipyards, where Hickson is a foreman, would make no further public statements concerning their story until they talked further with federal authorities.

Jackson County Chief Deputy Barney Mathis said the men told him they were fishing from an old pier on the west bank of Pascagoula River about 7 p.m. Thursday when they noticed a strange craft about two miles away emitting a bluish haze.

They said it moved closer and then appeared to hover about three or four feet above the water, then 'three what-ever-they-were came out, either floating or walking, and carried us into the ship', officers quoted Hickson as saying.

'The things had big eyes. They kept us about 20 minutes, photographed us and then took us back to the pier.

'The only sound they made was a buzzing-humming sound. They left in a flash.'

'These are reliable people,' Sheriff Fred Diamond said. 'They had no reason to say this if it had not been true. I know something did happen to them.'

The sheriff said the 'spacecraft' was described as fish-shaped, about 10 feet square with an eight-feet ceiling; the occupants were said to have pale silvery-gray skin, no hair, long pointed ears and noses with an opening for a mouth and hands like 'crab claws'.

Subsequently, the two men were interviewed by Dr. J. Allen Hynek, who is a professor of Astronomy at North Western University, and was civilian consultant to the former U.S. Air Force Project Blue Book, investigating UFOs, and also by a Dr. Harder of California. Hynek stated after examining the men under hypnosis that he found them 'telling the truth beyond a reasonable doubt'.

It seems more than likely that there are some UFOs that have bases under the seas, as both Sanderson and Jessup thought.

On 20 April, 1959, Dr. Morris K. Jessup was found dead. He had apparently committed suicide by inhaling carbon monoxide, presumably by connecting a hose to the exhaust of his station wagon and introducing it inside the vehicle.

Did Jessup know too much?

A very prominent scientist and leading ufologist was the late Dr. James E. McDonald, senior physicist, Institute of Atmospheric Physics, and Professor, Department of Meteorology, University of Arizona.

Dr. McDonald became a very outstanding speaker and writer on UFOs, and was very critical of the U.S. Air Force's handling of the UFO situation. Keel wrote that Dr. McDonald 'privately discussed, in his last years, the possibility that alien beings were not only present on this planet but were systematically taking over top posts in the government and military.[5]

On 13 June, 1971, his body was found in the desert north of Tucson, Arizona. He, too, had apparently done away with himself.

Did McDonald know too much?

Then there is the case of Professor René Hardy. He was a scientist of world repute; a prodigious inventor with over 250 patents in his name, in the fields of electronics, radio, television, ultrasonics and optics. He was interested in ufology, parapsychology and interstellar navigation, among many other subjects.

On 12 June, 1972, the Professor was found dead with a bullet in his head, and a revolver in his hand, just two days before he was to have announced a highly important discovery concerning space phenomena. There was no reason for his apparent suicide.

There followed a most extraordinary and significant happening. At the funeral of Professor Hardy there were six tall men that no one knew, and although photographs were taken of all present, *those six men did not appear in the printed photographs!*[6]

The suicides of Jessup, McDonald and Hardy may all have been perfectly genuine ones for personal reasons. However, it is certainly strange that three people, all of whom had played a leading part in ufology, should have left us in this most unfortunate manner.

It would seem that they knew too much about flying saucers (with apologies to Gray Barker).

24: Humming Sounds from Underground

During the past two decades strange humming noises, which seem to those that have heard them to be coming from underground, have been reported from different parts of the country.

These unexplained noises were heard about twenty years ago at Leigh-on-Sea, Essex, and also at Chalfont St. Giles, in Buckinghamshire. In more recent years the humming has been heard in the London area, down in Kent, and in Bournemouth.

The persistent humming at Chalfont St. Giles began in September, 1953, but by the end of the year the noise which had a deep vibration was becoming very loud. Some people were unable to get any sleep and lay awake listening to the constant humming which at times increased in intensity.

Harold T. Wilkins, in his book *Flying Saucers Uncensored,* mentions an unnamed correspondent who wrote him ...

of information he had got from a lady in the neighbourhood. Worried by the strange underground noises she heard, she had sought explanations from the local authorities. She was told they had none. The noises did *not* come from road work or pumping operations, or factory machinery. Examinations of 'victims' by a London specialist have disposed of the 'noises in the head' theory.

Wilkins's correspondent added:

'One difficulty is that only certain people hear the sounds. I, myself, could hear only a very faint throbbing; but, on the afternoon I called, Mrs. Craig told me it was not anywhere near as loud as it can be. She has very acute hearing, as also has the other lady, Mrs. Fielding. The mysterious sound is not high-pitched. Mrs. Craig describes it as resembling the sound of "giant wheels turning"...'[1]

After a very long time the humming eventually ceased at Chalfont St. Giles without the cause ever being located.

Some years later it started up again in the London area.

The *Evening Standard* for Thursday, 5 December, 1963, reported a mysterious humming sound that was causing people to be unable to sleep in a block of flats at Southfields.

The residents blamed generators in the LCC (as it then was) supplies depot nearby, but the LCC denied that there were any generators in the building.

The mystery was further accentuated by another report of people living about a mile away in Upper Richmond Road, Putney, who were having sleepless nights due to a humming sound.

Then, in the mid-1960s, many people in Kent, including, I recall, Mrs. Aylett Hyams, wife of author Edward Hyams, heard the hum which persisted for such a long period that some residents were unable to put up with it any longer, and actually moved from the area.

On 18 June, 1972, *The Sunday Express* printed a long news story about the hum which was now bothering the residents of Bournemouth! Whatever causes the hum seems to like a spot of travel.

Here is an extract from the newspaper report:

A mysterious high-pitched hum is plaguing people who live near Bournemouth. They say it is wearing down their nerves. And it alarms them even more because usually other members of their families cannot hear it.

One victim, Mr. Paul Wallace, 59-year-old translator, said 'Everyone who hears the noise agrees it's like having a dynamo in the head. It's a ringing hum, a vibration which is very painful.

'It gives me headaches and migraine and I can never get a good night's sleep because of it. Ear plugs seem to make it worse...'

The newspaper went on to report that Mr. Wallace was so desperate *after hearing the noise for five years*, that he had spent nearly £2,000 of his savings to pay an expert to find out what is causing the hum.

Now what does it all mean? Local authorities, electrical companies, the army, the air force, local factories, uncle Tom Cobley and all, deny being the cause of the hated hum.

These humming sounds seem to come from somewhere underground. A fantastic idea occurs to me: *Could it be that the inner Earth people are re-activating some of the Atlantean tunnel systems?*

25 : The Puma Mystery

Over the centuries, many strange and scientifically unacceptable animals, monsters, ape men and other weird creatures have appeared and been seen by large numbers of people all over the world.

There is an interesting parallel here with the UFOs which have also been seen throughout history.

During the last quarter of a century the number of sightings and encounters with these grotesque creatures has steadily increased. The number of UFO sightings and encounters with their occupants has also escalated over the same period to a fantastic degree.

Many ufologists now seriously consider that there is a link between the two phenomena.

Probably, the creature best known to the general public is the Yeti, more popularly known as 'The Abominable Snow Man'. Usually, the Yeti give off a horrible smell which is the reason for the nick-name. This creature has been seen in China, the Soviet Union and Tibet.

They vary in size from some three feet to ten feet or more, and the giant ones are covered in black hair, and have long arms.

The well-known American ufologist and writer, John A. Keel, tells of similar creatures in the United States, and how the Indians asserted 'that such creatures were ejected from "moons" which landed periodically in the valley'.[1]

Keel pointed out that many UFOs have been seen flying over Yeti-infested areas in the Himalayas.

In Canada, a similar creature to the Yeti has been frequently seen, and is known as the 'Sasquatch', an Indian name.

In the United States, the creatures are known as 'Big

Foot' and frequent, in particular, the states of California and Oregon.

Apart from these yeti-type creatures being seen in different parts of the world, there have been reported a number of unusual cat-like animals which seem to have a definite connection with the UFOs.

For many years, accounts have appeared in the British press of mystery 'pumas' that have been seen in England by farmers, police officers and other good folk. Reports of these elusive animals are not confined only to England. In fact, a veritable rash of them have been seen and encountered, both in the United States and Ireland.

Many UFOs have been reported in the areas, and at around the same time that the pumas have been seen. Once again, there appears to be a strong link between the two phenomena.

Incidentally, there is now an active organization in England called 'The Puma Research Group'. They have established a good liaison with the Hampshire police, and interview witnesses that sight pumas.[2] Their secretary, Mr. Cerris Francis, confirms that many of these puma sightings do occur during periods when there is UFO activity in a particular area.

Some years ago, Charles Bowen, the editor of *Flying Saucer Review*, wrote a full-length article in his magazine, called 'Mystery Animals', which tends to illustrate the point made of a connection with UFOs.[3]

One of the cases discussed by Mr. Bowen was that of farm manager, Edward Blanks, who had reported to the police that one of his steers had been savaged.

Bowen went to see him at Bushylease Farm and found the farmer a very down-to-earth type. The puma had been around the farm for about two years, and both Mr. and Mrs. Blanks, as well as their son, had caught sight of it at night.

Mr. Blanks told Bowen that it was his custom to make the rounds of his farm before retiring for the night.

On two occasions he suddenly became aware of a mysterious light on the roofs of the farm buildings. The light moved from roof to roof, yet he could not see the beam which produced the light. It was certainly not produced by car head-lights from the Odiham Road: the local topography precluded that possibility. Mr. Blanks could not trace the source of the light, and he was puzzled by the phenomenon, because on each occasion the mystery puma arrived on the scene shortly afterwards!

A very interesting case was reported on 6 July, 1966. Here it is from the London *Times*:

PUMA IS SEEN
STALKING A
RABBIT

From our Correspondent,
Guildford, July 4

The elusive puma that has been roaming the Surrey–Hampshire border for three years came out into the open today and was watched and followed by police, Post Office engineers and villagers for more than 20 minutes. The last shred of doubt among the police about its existence disappeared when it stalked and killed a rabbit in full view of a police inspector.

It appeared today in a meadow adjoining the home of the Queen's cousin, the Rev. Andrew Elphingstone, at Worplesdon, near Guildford, and among the first to see it was Inspector Eric Bourn, aged 55, of the Special Constabulary, who watched from his garden only 100 yards away.

Inspector Bourn said tonight that a Post Office engineer working 20 yards away yelled 'Look at that puma!'.

'I went to where he was standing and sure enough, without any doubt whatsoever, there was the puma. I watched it come out of a copse, and walk along the side of the meadow, keeping to the cover of the hedge, to within 100 yards of the bottom of my garden. Then it lay down out of sight. It was ginger-brown colour and the size of a labrador dog.'

CAT-LIKE FACE

'I rang the police. Just as they arrived it got up and sauntered back at a leisurely pace to the copse as I watched through field glasses. I do not know whether it saw us watching but it was in no hurry as it went into Mr. Elpingstone's copse and disappeared. We went over to where it had lain in the grass and found a half-eaten rabbit.'

A motorcycle patrol officer, Police Constable Robin Young, said:

'The animal was in sight for 20 minutes and there was no doubt that it was the puma. It was ginger-coloured and had a long tail with a white tip and a cat-like face. It was just walking casually round the meadow. I had a good look at it through binoculars from 60 yards away.

'One of the villagers there had a shotgun and took a pot shot. Then the animal took off. We followed it for about half a mile and then lost it when it reached the road.'

There have been many other puma sightings, both before and since *The Times* account just related. These have been reported in both the press and in *Flying Saucer Review*.[4]

These mystery cats have also been encountered in Ireland, the Soviet Union and the U.S.A.

It is true that the mountain lion is indigenous to certain mountain areas in the United States but these puma-like animals have been seen many times in that country far from the natural habitat of the mountain lion.

UFO researchers will recall the famous Socorro, New Mexico landing on 24 April, 1964, involving police officer Lonnie Zamora.[5] Numerous oval-shaped, or cat-paw-like markings were found around the scorched area where the UFO had landed.

Two American ufologists, Jerome Clark and Loren Coleman, wrote a two-part article in the U.S. magazine, *Fate*, called 'On the Trail of Pumas, Panthers and ULAs (unidentified leaping animals)'.[6]

The writers described many puma sightings. However, they brought out the interesting point that cat-like animals have often been seen in connection with UFO 'flaps'. Even the 1896–97 UFO flap in the U.S.A. coincided with the appearance of these mystery animals! The fact is that it is not just in England that the puma phenomena seem to coincide with UFO activity.

Charles Bowen ended his article 'Mystery Animals', mentioned earlier, by asking:

Where do these animals come from? Certainly not zoos and circuses, for no such losses have been reported. It seems highly unlikely that a number of private persons have had cheetahs and pumas as domestic pets which they cannot report as lost because they smuggled them into the country in the first place. So I repeat, where do they come from, and what is their purpose?

Where do they come from? Although the puma is not indigenous to England, it certainly is to this planet. If there is a connection with the UFO phenomena, which seems highly probable from the evidence available, then it does not seem logical for these animals to be flown here across millions of miles from some other planet or planets. In any case, the evolution of animal life on other planets may have taken quite a different course from that on Earth.

The puma, it should be emphasized, is indigenous to this planet. A strong case has been advocated in this book for the existence of a hollow Earth and for the UFOs coming into our atmosphere from entrances in the polar areas.

Therefore, it seems much more likely that the ufonauts, for reasons best known to themselves, are landing pumas, and perhaps other creatures, on different parts of the Earth's surface from the interior of the Earth.

UFOs have been reported throughout history. Generally speaking, these were spasmodic events. However, nearer to our own times there was a big 'flap' of cigar-shaped objects over the U.S.A. in 1897, and two more 'flaps', one over Britain in 1909 and another over New Zealand later the same year.[1]

It may have been a coincidence, but when the Bomb was let off over Japan in 1945, the UFOs really began to get around and have been seen since by millions of people all over the world.

In a magazine article some years ago I suggested that as a result of our nuclear activity a chain reaction might be set off affecting other solar systems in the galaxy, and that that was the reason for the sudden influx of UFOs in our atmosphere. In short, that these space craft were coming from other planets and solar systems to observe what was going on here.

Shortly afterwards, my good friend, Señor Antonio Ribera, a leading Spanish ufologist, took me to task for suggesting that our nuclear activity could upset the equilibrium of the galaxy.[2]

He pointed out that the galaxy has withstood much worse cataclysms than our comparatively puny nuclear explosions. For example, the explosion of the supernova which created the Crab Nebula and the fifteen novae seen with the naked eye since 1900. He emphasized that these *were* explosions in a very real sense but did not cause the galaxy to lose its balance.

It is much nearer home that the reason will be found for the UFOs' suddenly increased appearances after the Bomb was detonated.

The people most concerned, apart from ourselves, would be those living inside the Earth. They might well be perturbed by our underground explosions and, indeed, by radioactive fall-out from our overhead explosions entering their tunnels. If inner Earth people have a technology far more advanced than our own, then they certainly would know of the dangers nuclear activity on the surface could bring them.

I have already referred to von Daniken's theory that the giant tunnels under Ecuador and Peru were built as vast shelters in which to take refuge, in case of attack from outer space. His theory could equally well be applied to all the other cyclopean tunnels mentioned in this book around the world.

Earlier, too, reference has been made to the 'thunderbolts' thrown by Zeus and the other gods, and of other death-dealing weapons. It is more than likely that the Atlanteans had something akin or even more lethal than nuclear weapons at their disposal, so when we started our nuclear explosions in 1945 and onward, the inhabitants of the inner Earth, knowing what could come of our activities in this direction, may well have been alarmed.

Over and over again, contactees have been given messages for mankind by flying saucer pilots, telling us to stop nuclear activity. It is well worth repeating the question: if it is not visitors from outer space that are worried about our nuclear activity, then who would be most concerned about it? The answer undoubtedly points to those people that live under the surface of this planet.

It is appreciated that a great deal of the material in the second part of this book reads like incidents out of a James Bond thriller. The 'Men in Black', the 'foreign-looking' men that suddenly appear at UFO landing sites and the secretive nocturnal visits of flying saucers unloading pumas in isolated country districts. It all seems to add up to some 'undercover' military operation. Indeed, for a long time now, most ufologists have accepted that UFOs based near the Earth (very few have dared to suggest inside it) are potentially hostile. This viewpoint is based upon the secretive and evasive actions of the UFOs and their occupants.

In my previous books the Sky People have always been presented as friendly towards humanity. This, I still believe. The real Sky People will be discussed later.

The majority of UFOs seen in our atmosphere come from an area pertaining to our planet. That is now the accepted view of most leading ufologists. It is those particular UFOs that are regarded with some suspicion.

The descendants of the original people that went inside the Earth may look reasonably like us. It could be that the surface of our planet is being gradually infiltrated by inner Earth people for some purpose. Keel mentioned that the late Dr. McDonald had ideas on the same lines, though no doubt the Doctor may have considered the aliens to be coming from somewhere out in space.

If there is any truth in this conjecture, then it would be most unlikely that these people would be coming from space. Though it is quite conceivable that there is intelligent life in deep space, and that other planets have been seeded by some highly advanced civilization in the same way that our own planet was long, long ago, it is not really feasible that intelligent beings on other planets would have evolved in exactly the same way as human beings here.

The people who would look most like us would be the people living inside the Earth. Some inner Earth people could have been living on the surface for some considerable time. When others are dropped here by UFOs, those inner Earth people already living here could meet them and provide the necessary papers.

Keel has called this undercover activity 'Operation Trojan Horse', and in a remarkable book under that title has amplified the whole clandestine work as being directed by 'Ultra-Terrestrials'.[3] In his book he has done some splendid objective reporting of these undercover operations, but because many of the incidents include psychic overtones and the use of extrasensory perception (ESP) by the visitors, then according to Keel (and his view is shared by many ufologists), the phenomena must originate from 'ultra-terrestrials' in an invisible universe. This idea, if the inner Earth is inhabited, is not necessarily valid. At the same time, it should not be discounted, either.

If the hollow Earth exists, then the interior must be a physical area like the surface of the planet. The inhabitants could be the descendants of a race or races who originally lived on the surface, and who built such amazing structures as the Gate of the Sun at Tiahuanaco, close to Lake Titicaca, 12,000 feet up in the High Andes, on the borders of Peru and Bolivia; the platform at Baalbeck, to the north-east of Beirut in the Lebanon, upon which the Romans much later built with 200-ton stones! Our present much-vaunted civil-Easter Island; and the Fortress of Secsahuaman, in Peru, built with 200-ton stones! Our present much-vaunted civil-ization could not build such edifices today.

The civilization existing on this planet before cata-strophe struck must have been a spectacular one. The remains of its fantastic buildings in different parts of the world and the discovery of the Piri Re'is map prove it.

It is highly probable that a civilization of that calibre would have been capable of constructing space craft of the types that we call UFOs. In addition to their technological and scientific ability, it is more than possible that ancient civilizations had developed paranormal powers and were capable of performing many feats that most people would term 'magical'.

Some people may scoff at this last suggestion, but re-member that we live in a material age; especially those who live in the western world. In India and Tibet there are many yogis possessing similiar abilities.

H. T. Wilkins, in his book *Flying Saucers Uncensored*, included a letter from his friend, Frederick G. Hehr, an engineer and traveller, who was then residing at Santa Monica, California. Here is an extract from it:

My opinion is that the saucers look for 'markers' scattered all over the world in far past ages. Some of these 'markers' must have grown dim. They are in straight lines and about fifty miles apart. One was found in Oregon, when some guy set up an assay office over the spot and was nearly shot because his assays differed widely from those taken outside.

No, I do not think that flying saucers are 'etheric'. If they were, they would not be visible. I think they are totally shielded by a force field against mass and gravity. This may explain their brilliance and mathematical form and perfect finish. Others who have seen some of them at slow speed have noted a material formation with lack of this utter perfection. In my opinion, the saucers are left-overs from one of the Atlantean civilizations, and there may be a few from a Lemurian civilization.[4]

Too true, a race of people who went inside the Earth at the time of the Atlantean catastrophe may well be sending up the flying saucers that are seen in our skies.

This, then, is the Third Choice which should be seriously considered by ufologists and every thinking person, in addition to the extra-terrestrial theory, and a vague invisible area interpenetrating our planet so much now in vogue.

27: Is There a 'Fifth Column' Among Us?

Another disturbing phenomenon is the vast number of people that disappear every year. Some people make themselves scarce for the usual mundane reasons. For example, to escape from their wives or husbands, the tax man and the police. However, the majority disappear without a trace for no apparent reason at all. According to Keel, 100,000 people disappear in the U.S.A. every year.[1]

What have these disappearances to do with UFOs?

The significant answer is that most of these disappearances take place during UFO flaps!

It would appear that the ufonauts have a very great knowledge of people on the surface of this planet and, in some cases, go to great trouble to take those with special qualifications that might be of use to them, even to the extent of rescuing such a person from drowning.

The following newspaper report appeared in the *Listin Diario* of 28 October, 1972, and was included in an article by Salvador Freixedo called 'UFOs Over the Caribbean', published in *Flying Saucer Review Case Histories*.[2]

It is nine o'clock in the morning. On a deserted road near San Cristobal a man appears and flags down a car. The driver, an insurance company director whom we shall call X.X., slows down and pulls up. The man approaches. He is wearing a sort of light-green overall with a shiny glint to it. The garment covers his feet. He is wearing no shoes, no gloves, and has no pockets, no weapons, no insignia. It is noted that he is wearing a sort of watch on his left wrist.

This mysterious person asks X.X.: 'Don't you know me?'

'No,' says X.X.

'My name is F— M—,' says the man. (This is the name of a person well known in Santo Domingo, who disappeared mysteriously in the sea about fifteen years ago.)

The mystery visitor continues: 'It was thought that I was drowned along with two other people. But I was rescued by a modern machine.'

X.X. 'By a helicopter?'

F.M. 'No. Supposedly a module, that is to say, what you folks call a U.F.O. I was rescued by these two people (he points towards two companions a certain distance away) because of my knowledge of radio techniques and my intelligence.'

The two people mentioned are over 6ft. high, slim and dressed in identical fashion to F.M. Their hair is short and brown, and their skin a light colour, like that of the Chinese. They remain silent, standing there with arms crossed, observing the scene.

F.M. draws the attention of X.X. to the machine in which they have come. It is of the size of an automobile, has the shape of an American football, and its surface is nickelled.

X.X. 'What are they doing here?'

F.M. 'Supposedly investigating.'

X.X. 'What sort of investigating?'

F.M. 'Investigating.'

X.X. 'From where do they come?'

F.M. 'Supposedly from Venus.'

The stranger adds that they are greatly interested in the Milwaukee grave.

Then F.M. says: 'Step back. We are about to leave.'

The dialogue has lasted some five minutes. Just as the three individuals are about to depart, F.M. turns round and tells X.X. not to worry if his car won't start at once. He says everything will return to normality.

Mr. Gordon Creighton, who translated Salvador Freixedo's article for the magazine, commented in a footnote regarding the phrase 'La fosa de Milwaukee':

I confess that at first I was utterly stumped by this, but now, as a postscript, I can add that this is not a grave, or archaeological relic in Milwaukee, U.S.A., but the name of an Ocean Deep which is part of the Puerto Rico Trench.

One fact sticks out like a sore thumb after studying this

dialogue, and that is the general evasiveness of F.M.'s replies.

When F.M. is asked where the three men have come from, the reply is 'supposedly from Venus'. The inference being that that is where many ufologists think the UFOs originate. *However, he does not directly answer the question.*

Then, when F.M. is asked what they are doing here, the reply is 'supposedly investigating'. When pressed to be more specific, the answer is 'investigating'. It is true that F.M. adds they are interested in the Milwaukee grave, though that could well be a 'red herring'.

What really intrigues one is why F.M., who was a native of this planet, now behaves in such an evasive and secretive manner. It is almost as if he had been 'brain-washed'!

Another staggering thought arises from the case of F.M. *Will we, one fine day, discover that thousands of the people who have disappeared from the face of the Earth are now living inside the planet, 'brain-washed' by some hypnotic machine, and subservient to their new masters!*

Perhaps the people who disappear (or are abducted), after being 'brain-washed', are sent back to the surface with special work to do for the inner Earth people.

During the Second World War, the term 'fifth column' was used for any organization in a country that was actively assisting the enemy. *There may be an active fifth column already here among us.*

No doubt, some people will consider that a gloomy and perhaps sinister picture has been painted in the second part of this book. Maybe they are right. However, there are many strange facets to the UFO story. It is neither scientific nor honest to sweep certain reports and facts 'under the carpet'. This subject cannot be looked at through rose-coloured spectacles.

Possibly, the bizarre happenings described in the last few chapters are all illusory, though they are well documented.

Maybe there are no mysterious 'Men in Black', and all the UFO researchers who have been 'silenced' were just paranoid.

Perhaps the Yeti, the Sasquatch, the Big Foot and the Surrey–Hampshire puma don't exist. After all, police officers are human, just like us. Maybe they made a mistake in stating the puma was real. However, these cat-like animals have been seen by police officers in the U.S.A., too. And it is well verified that these animals appear during UFO flaps.

Yes, it all certainly does add up to a disturbing picture. However, the early classical writers stated that the 'Abode of the Gods' was in the centre of the Earth, and that this was a Paradise indeed.

Therefore, you must 'pay your penny and take your choice', as to whether the inhabitants of the interior of the Earth are for or against us.

We live today in a time of increasing turbulence and violence. Hijackings, kidnappings and skulduggery are commonplace occurrences, reported daily in our newspapers.

In an article written some time ago I likened the state of this planet to an empty ink bottle. Some occultists and mystics believe that invisible energies are pouring in on us which have a strange effect. They make those that are inclined to do violence more violent; and those that are slanted towards a spiritual way of life more spiritual. If you like, this process could be called the 'sorting of the wheat from the chaff'.

Let us continue with the analogy of the ink bottle. When you pour in fresh water, all the dirty muck lying at the bottom of the bottle rises to the top, and a similar situation is occurring right now on this planet. The muck – that is, the violence; the increasing crime; the drug scene; the permissive society and political scandals, all of which are part and parcel of this picture.

It is my belief that this planet, like the ink bottle in this analogy, will suddenly become cleansed and all the muck will disappear.

Then, we may see the re-appearance of the real Sky People who have been waiting in the wings before venturing once again on to the Earth's stage.

Keel has pointed out that 666, 'the mark of the beast', inverted becomes 999.[1] According to biblical prophecy the 'beast' has to be loosened first.

Prophecy is a very dubious business. However, in *Operation Earth* reference was made to Nostradamus who has more 'bull's-eyes' to his credit than any other seer!

Michel de Nostredame, known as Nostradamus, was friend and adviser to Queen Catherine de Medici. He wrote his predictions down in more than 900 quatrains. There is a particularly well-known one about an event to take place in 1999:

> In the year 1999 and seven months
> From the skies shall come an
>   alarmingly powerful king,
> To raise again the great King of
>   the Jacquerie.
> Before and after, Mars shall reign
>   at Will.

Now, the French word *Jacquerie* is one that was in common usage before and during the time of Nostradamus. The word meant peasants, or the common people as a whole.

Here is a quote from *Operation Earth*:

Now the choice of words in this quatrain is extremely interesting. Nostradamus does not say that a great King of the Jacquerie will be set up or instigated. He states quite clearly that the powerful king from the skies shall come '*To raise again the great King of the Jacquerie*'.

In short, there has already been one or more before, and this office is going to be resurrected or reinstated! Now, readers of an earlier book, *Men Among Mankind*, will be familiar with the dual system of rulership that was in being when the inhabitants of Earth were in open contact with Sky People aeons ago. There was an off-planet ruler who was the Priest King or Divine Ruler, and also, a secular ruler from our own planet who looked after administration and day-to-day affairs here.

When the Sky People left after the sinking of Atlantis, this dual system was carried on symbolically in Ancient Egypt until the time of Menes.

This prediction by Nostradamus that the 'alarmingly powerful king' from the skies is going to raise again the King of the Jacquerie is a clear indication that the Sky People upon their return are going once more to re-introduce this dual system of rulership.[2,3]

It would seem that although the Earth has a very difficult time to go through for some years ahead, the long-term future looks better. That is, if we go along with Nostradamus, but comfort can be taken from the knowledge that he was the most successful of all seers into the future.

The human race may one day become welcome members of what Sir Fred Hoyle has referred to as the 'galactic telephone directory'.[4] Furthermore, our descendants may enjoy wonders beyond our wildest dreams and journey to the stars.

29 : A Military Operation

There are many indications that most of the flying saucers come from inside the Earth, and that a large, well-planned operation is being carried out by the ufonauts.

Earlier, it was stated that the UFOs during the last 25 years have been dropping earthly substances on our soil. That is, aluminium, silicon, magnesium, calcium and other chemicals. Why they should drop all this material is not at all clear but like everything else in this jig-saw puzzle, there is probably a very good reason for it. Maybe, they regard the surface of our planet as a suitable place to drop their garbage! Seriously though, the fact that they are leaving behind earthly substances is another pointer that their origin is not in outer space.

Then, an account has been given of the mysterious humming sounds that have been heard for long periods – in some instances lasting several years – coming from underground, and these noises may well have something to do with the activities of inner Earth people.

Let us now summarize the strange undercover operations of the ufonauts.

Firstly, there are the 'foreign-looking' men who dress like us, and turn up at a UFO landing site, often before eye-witnesses have had time to report the incident.

You will recall that in the second part of this book, when discussing the launching of the early satellites, it was explained that personnel would be waiting at the calculated spot worked out by technicians, to pick up the nose cones.

It is highly likely that most UFO landings are planned beforehand. Therefore, it would be quite conceivable for the inner Earth people to have representatives here on the surface; some of these would be at the landing spot at a prearranged time. A number of subsurface people have probably been living on the surface for years. Indeed, they may have had spies among us for thousands of years.

Harold T. Wilkins, in *Flying Saucers Uncensored*, wrote:

My query is: HAVE THE SAUCERS TERRESTRIAL SPIES AND CONTACTS?
I conclude that they may have! ... Fantastic as it sounds, one might speculate whether there may have been, and still be, something in the nature of a secret society which, in the last five or six centuries, may have established such contacts, and maintained them to this day ...[1]

The fact that these representatives turn up at many landing sites is indicative of a well-planned, big operation. It is true that these strange men have not always been seen on such occasions, but perhaps ufonauts are allowed sometimes to make a spot landing for some other motive.

Secondly, consider the 'Men in Black' who frightened Bender into closing down his organization. They have silenced, harassed and threatened many other UFO researchers throughout the world.

Who are these mysterious 'Men in Black'? The answer to that one is that they are the equivalent of intelligence operatives from the inner world. Every so often, they call on some UFO researcher who has got too close to the truth.

It is interesting that they always dress in black, which is the colour of the dark or negative forces. Incidentally, clergymen wear black clothes, too. Now, I wonder what is the reason for that. Anyway, the 'Men in Black' are another part of the big undercover operation.

Thirdly, there is the landing of pumas and possibly other creatures in various countries. These pumas have been landed at night, and it is a well-attested fact that sightings of them have coincided with UFO 'flaps' in the same areas.

Pumas are not indigenous to some of the countries in which they have been seen. For example, England and

Ireland are not their natural habitats. They are, however, indigenous to our planet, and not necessarily to another world.

Therefore, the Earth being hollow, with very likely a subtropical temperature, it is reasonable to assume that this is where these 'out of place' pumas originated.

Another fantastic, but perfectly feasible, idea has just made its way through my 'little grey cells'. In an earlier chapter the brain-washing of surface people was suggested. Perhaps the inner Earth people with the aid of their hypnotic machines could programme the pumas to do a job of work on the surface.

Now, that really is an idea! Not so crazy when you think about it. Possibly, the first thing to do would be to establish a considerable rapport with the puma. Well, we have made a fair amount of progress in communicating with the dolphin.

Then, with the aid of the machines, the animals could be programmed for whatever work is required. In short, the puma would be landed from a UFO under the cover of darkness; go about its programmed business, and at an arranged time, the UFO would return at night to pick up the waiting animal.

Some readers may consider the idea of pumas being programmed for special work as too fanciful. However, as *The Daily Telegraph* reported in their issue of 1 February, 1974, at a symposium organized by the British Small Animals' Veterinary Association, this very idea was highlighted by Dr. Boris Levinson, Professor of Psychology at Touro College, New York, a specialist on relations between human beings and animals.

Later, at his London hotel, Dr. Levinson told the newspaper's reporter that it is only a question of time before small electrodes can be put into every part of animals' brains to make them do anything.

Fourthly, the idea was broached that people from the inner Earth might be infiltrating and taking over responsible posts in some of our governmental and military departments. In particular, Keel mentioned Dr. James McDonald's view that alien visitors were actually doing this.

Apparently, Dr. McDonald considered that people from outer space were infiltrating into these responsible posts, but it seems much more likely that inner Earth people, who know everything about us and resemble surface people, would be more suitable candidates than extra-terrestrials. This could also have been going on for a very long time. In fact, it would make it much easier for them to take us over when the time is ripe. All part of the big operation.

Fifthly, the idea of a 'Fifth Column' operating on the surface of our planet was discussed. In support of this suggestion, there is the case of F.M. who was rescued from drowning by the ufonauts. You will recall F.M. was wanted by them because of his intelligence and knowledge of radio techniques. Now he is working for them.

Then, linking up with this last example, there is the vast number of people who disappear off the surface of our planet every year. Some disappear for obvious reasons but a very large number just go for no apparent motive, and leave no trace. It is my belief that many of these missing people have been abducted and taken to the inner world.

The inner Earth people are taking away large numbers of our world population, brain-washing and programming them to work for them; either on the surface or in the interior of the Earth. This is a very big part of the operation.

The clandestine UFO activity and landings at night show that these craft are coming for some secret purpose. *Surely, if these people in the UFOs were from some invisible, psychic realm, then there would be no need for them to use space craft at all; especially when all this UFO activity takes place at night, which indicates a desire not to be seen.*

It would seem that all these bizarre and sinister actions are leading up to some big event. The manner in which they are being carried out is reminiscent of a military operation.

The Bible tells us something interesting about inner Earth
people coming to the surface of the planet:

> And they had a king over them,
> Which is the angel of the bottomless pit,
> Whose name in the Hebrew tongue is
> Abaddon, but in the Greek tongue
> hath his name Apollyon.
> Saying to the sixth angel which had
> the trumpet, Loose the four angels
> which are bound in the great river
> Euphrates.

Revelation 9: 11, 14

In the first part of this book, it was stated that according
to Greek mythology, traditionally Hades had four rivers
flowing through it. These were the Styx, the Acheron, the
Phlegeton and the Cocytus.

It would seem from the verses quoted from *Revelation*
that despite the fact that there is a River Euphrates on the
surface of our planet, reference is being made to another
one inside the Earth. Palmer commented about the mean-
ing of these two verses, as follows:

The Euphrates is one of the four great rivers which flow out
of Eden. If we look at the globe, we will find that the oceans
are parted into four major sections by land masses surrounding
the Pole. Since the other three rivers mentioned in Genesis as
emerging from Eden (Pi-son, Gi-hon and Hi-de-kel – Author)
have never been found, and the Euphrates of today has failed
to give us a clue as to the location of Eden through lack of the
other rivers, might we conclude that the four angels are to be
loosed from a river inside the Earth under the domination of
Abaddon?

Indeed, the succeeding verses in the same chapter of *Revelation* relate of a veritable army coming forth against us.

Jess Stearn in his book, *The Door to the Future*, wrote:

It is interesting to note that both Jeane Dixon and the late Edgar Cayce have predicted a threat to America through the Davis Strait, that little-travelled passage between Greenland and the mainland of North America, from which an over-the-pole attack could conceivably be launched. 'I don't know why it should be,' Mrs. Dixon remarked, 'but that is a vulnerable area.' Perhaps this is warning to the wise.[1]

The late Edgar Cayce and Mrs. Jeane Dixon will probably go down in history as the two most successful seers of modern times.

It is likely that both of them 'saw' a slant-eyed race coming from the north and concluded that the threat was from China. In another part of Stearn's book, Mrs. Dixon mentions China as the potential enemy.

A noteworthy point is that both the Eskimo and the Chinese are slant-eyed peoples, and both have legends of coming out of the Earth in the long and distant past. There are, also, many stories of inner Earth people having slanted eyes. This may well have something to do with living in that particular environment.

In this book, it has been shown that the ufonauts are carrying out some strange operations on the surface of our planet. Most ufologists are of the opinion that the majority of the ufonauts should be considered as potentially hostile. This opinion is based upon a study of UFO landings, nocturnal activity and the general deceitfulness, evasiveness and trickery of the ufonauts themselves, combined with their obvious desire not to be seen on certain occasions.

Many people today think that there will shortly be a final confrontation between the forces of Good and Evil. There is no doubt at all that we are approaching a climax in the history of Mankind. The tempo of life is moving too fast.

Something will have to slow it up and bring the world back to reality. That something could be a conflict between inner Earth and surface people for the ownership of this planet. If that happened, it would unite all the countries of this troubled world as never before, in one common cause.

31: Postscript

The closing weeks of 1973 have seen a tremendous UFO 'flap' in the United States, coupled with many sightings around the world. This is probably the biggest ever rash of UFO activity that has occurred to date, and may be heralding some big event. There have been both sighting and landing reports on a vast scale, as well as much activity from our charming 'Men in Black'. The UFOs have recently been seen by people in all walks of life, including police officers, and for good measure by no less a person than the Governor of the State of Ohio, Mr. John Gilligan.

Four men in a U.S. Army helicopter encountered a UFO on Thursday, 18 October. The Commander of the 'copter, Captain Larry Coyne, reported that the UFO was heading for them at a speed of 600 miles per hour.

Coyne took immediate evasive action and put the helicopter into a sudden dive. Then, a most startling thing happened. The UFO, travelling at a speed of 600 miles per hour, suddenly slowed to 100 miles per hour – just like that – which was the speed of the helicopter, and hovered at about 500 feet above them. After a few seconds the UFO turned and went off at a great speed.

Captain Coyne then set about pulling the helicopter out of its dive.

It was then that the startled crew discovered one of the most freakish aspects of the episode.

At the moment the UFO had swooped overhead, the helicopter was at an altitude of 1,500 and going down.

Now, seconds later, it was 3,800 feet high in the air! ...[1]

This was a complete impossibility for the machine to do of its own accord.

On 29 November, 1973, BBC Radio 4 reported that half the Americans interviewed in a Gallup Poll – 51 per cent – regarded unidentified flying objects (UFOs) as real and not imaginary. This is a fantastic increase on the previous poll.

Parallel with the tremendous increase of believers in UFOs there is a growing interest in paranormal subjects. That is, telepathy and various aspects of what is called extra-sensory perception, such as clairaudience, telekenisis, clairvoyance and astrology, among others.

There is an unfortunate side to this growth. In the United States, and to a lesser extent in the United Kingdom, there has been a corresponding increase of both interest and participation in witchcraft, black magic and the activities of vampires. All this, of course, is on the negative side of the coin. Perhaps I should not have mentioned witchcraft in this connection, as the real wizards and witches were and are working positively. However, they would be the first to admit that a lot of 'phoneys' and undesirables have got on their particular 'bandwagon' and are practising black magic arts, bringing the old witchcraft into disrepute. I would suggest that this influence comes from inside the Earth and emanates from Satanaku's caverns. In previous books I have pointed out that each and every one of us is responsible for our own destiny, but I must qualify that by pointing out that it is very easy for the inner Earth people with their machines and advanced powers of ESP to influence us on the surface. I know that this is a very controversial suggestion but believe it to be true. However, those that know how to 'protect' themselves through higher spiritual understanding are not influenced by these evil forces but many weak-minded people are easy prey to what Shaver calls the 'Deros'.

Let me give an example of the growing interest in paranormal subjects. The *Daily Telegraph* colour magazines dated 30 November and 7 December, 1973, respectively, carried several articles in both issues on the human aura, the undefined sixth sense, astrology, faith healing, ESP and a feature on the amazing Uri Geller.

Millions of people either saw the young Israeli on television, heard him on radio or have read about his feats in the press.

Now I must be one of the odd men out in this day and age as I do not have a television set. However, so many of my friends who watched Geller on TV told me not only of the most extraordinary demonstration of psychokinetic abilities on the screen but also of strange things happening in their own homes.

I would like to quote an extract from a recent communication from a friend of mine, Mrs. Marilyn Preston, who happens to be a remarkable healer and lives at Saltash in Cornwall. She wrote:

In a recent television programme with David Dimbleby in his 'Talk-In' series, we watched as the 'impossible' happened, and how Uri's thoughts were able to attune to some power ... which resulted in not only cutlery bending and breaking in the studio, but also, as on the Jimmy Young Show, of similar things happening in homes all over the country at that same instant. Reports from many parts of the country poured in to say watches and clocks had stopped, or broken ones had suddenly started, spoons and knives were bending and curling in amazed folks' homes and police in some counties contacted the BBC to report 'unnatural happenings'...

What Uri Geller was demonstrating in a most effective manner was what we should all be able to do quite naturally. Due to our material civilization, the 'rat race' and our present sophisticated way of living, our extra-sensory powers, latent in us all, have got completely atrophied.

Today, we rely so much on material techniques. For example, the telephone, the cable service, telex and, of course, the spoken and written word for communication purposes; so, telepathy, the facility of transferring thoughts and messages from one person to another over short or long distances, has become a lost gift.

I think that Uri Geller, with demonstrations of his fantastic mental abilities, has given people, both here and in America, something akin to a traumatic shock. In fact, he has done more to shake people out of their mental lethargy and to make them think than the churches have done over the last few centuries.

Scientists are absolutely baffled by Uri's abilities but are so interested in his performances that they want to test him under laboratory conditions. Both the Max Planck Institute in Munich, Germany, and the Stanford Research Institute in California, have set up experiments to test Uri's psychic and telepathic abilities. Some of these tests have already been undertaken and the Israeli has emerged with flying colours.

There have, of course, always been people with remarkable spiritual and mental powers in this world. Uri has stated that he is not a magician in the usual sense of the word. He claims that his abilities come from God. Well, God-power is latent in all of us but as stated earlier this has fallen into disuse, and only lip service is paid to our source.

Uri Geller is possibly an example of what Teilhard de Chardin called 'the ultra-human' that is now emerging on our planet.[2] There are others, but the difference is that Uri has demonstrated his abilities on television both here and in the United States. He is telling us really that we can do those things too, just as a great teacher 2,000 years ago said, 'What I can do you can do.'

Now, don't get me wrong. Uri does not pretend to be the Christ or anything like that. He is just demonstrating the powers that the teacher told us were our heritage.

We must not forget, too, that the evil forces can use the same powers for negative purposes and this is being done today. Biblical prophecy tells us that the Anti-Christ will arrive and rule the world before the Christ returns.

Satanaku's forces are still inside the Earth. If you accept Richard S. Shaver's stories, then they are already manipulating our thoughts, causing wars, assassinations, crimes and all sorts of skulduggery on the surface. Many assassins have said afterwards that 'God told them to stab' someone. There are many other examples of this nature.

The old machines of Atlantis are still there inside the Earth, intact and indestructible. They have apparatus that can see through solid rock. This is not impossible as our own scientists are getting towards this ability themselves with the aid of lasers and other remarkable discoveries.

It is my firm view that the ground work has now been prepared for a take-over of this planet by those who live inside it. A great deal has already been accomplished. They have their representatives here, many in high places. Then, the Anti-Christ, Satanaku, long prophesied, will rule the world – the whole planet, both inside and on the surface, until Armageddon. It is my belief, and once again according to biblical prophecy (which has never been wrong), that eventually Christ will return with his Angels (who are the real Sky People).

Meanwhile, please ponder over whether our natural spaceship, the planet Earth, is hollow and inhabited. I have given you proof that it is. If the answer to these questions in your own mind is in the affirmative, then this must surely be the *Secret of the Ages*.

PERSONAL STATEMENT

The theme of this book is very unusual. Therefore, it is only right that I should state that the ideas and views expressed are my own, and not necessarily those of Contact International, a world-wide movement, of which I have the honour to be President, nor of the British U.F.O. Research Association who have kindly made me one of their Vice-Presidents.

The Author

CONTACT INTERNATIONAL: THE LARGEST UFO MOVEMENT IN THE WORLD

The aims of Contact International are to collect, collate and analyse reports of UFO sightings, landings and other allied incidents, on a world-wide scale. To explore and study all possible theories as to who and what the UFOs and their occupants are; why they are coming here, and from where they originate. Membership is open to all people of any colour, race or religion.

President and Chairman of International Committee
   The Hon. Brinsley Le Poer Trench.
International Advisory Council
   Vice-Presidents:
      Captain Ivar Mackay (U.K.)
      Frank van Vloten (South Africa)
   International Research Officer:
      D. N. Mansell.
   International Public Relation Officers:
      Miss Ruth Rees
      J. B. Delair
      Dr. John Cleary-Baker, Ph.D
      F. W. Passey
      R. Stanway, F.R.A.S., M.B.A.
Member countries and addresses of international committee members. If you reside in these listed countries write to the addresses given for details of membership.

ARGENTINE: Professor Richard A. Frondizi, Hipolito Yrigoyen 3560. 8°. 24 Buenos Aires.
AUSTRALIA: K. McGuffin, 2, Iredale Street, Newtown, N.S.W. 2042.
BANGLADESH: M. Habibullah Bahar, Barisal Rest House Building, 14 Clay Road, Khulna.
BELGIUM: Comtesse R. d'Oultremont, 'Val des Pins', 26, Drève du Château, Linkebeek.

CANADA: J. B. Musgrave, 10510 86th Avenue, Edmonton, Alberta, T6E 2M6.

CHANNEL ISLANDS: Allen Palmer, 24, Maison St. Louis, St. Saviour, Jersey.

COLOMBIA: Albert Ron, Apartado Aereo 1320, Cali, Valle.

CUBA: Professor Moshe Asis, Rabi 655, La Habana 5.

CYPRUS: E. A. L. Coudounaris, P.O. Box 2405, Nicosia.

EIRE: Fergus Roche, 6 Drombawn Avenue, Dublin, 9.

FRANCE: Monsieur J. C. Salemi, 26, Rue Louis-Blanc, Saint-Leu-La-Foret, 95, Val d'Oise.

HOLLAND: Miss C. J. de Witte, v. Langsbergenstr. 64, s. Gravenhage, Den Haag.

HONG KONG: Henry Chan, 39, Tin Chin Street, Flat 405, North Point.

NEW ZEALAND: P. R. Austin, P.O. Box 10-151, Balmoral, Auckland 4.

NIGERIA: Dr. O. E. Hogen, Box 19, Nwaniba via Uyo, South Eastern State.

NORWAY: Nils Jacob Jacobsen, Disenveien 15, 111, Oslo 5.

PHILIPPINES: N. A. Villarruz, 104, Roxas Avenue, Roxas City.

PUERTO RICO: Noel E. Rigau, 855, Las Marias Avenue, Rio Pedras, Puerto Rico—00927.

SINGAPORE: Sahrom bin jalil, 2 Eber Road, Singapore, 9.

SLOVENIA (Yugoslavia): Milos Krmelj, Milcinskega 6, Llubljana 61000, Slovenija.

SOUTH AFRICA: F. Van Vloten, P.O. Box 743, Durban, Natal.

SPAIN: Señor Antonio Ribera, Calle Barcelona 42, San Feliu de Codinas, Barcelona.

SRI LANKA: Upali Amarasena, 'Amarani', Galboda, Indurawa.

SWEDEN: Mrs. Edith C. M. Nicolaisen, Parthenon, Halsingborg, 5.

TRINIDAD AND TOBAGO: Leo L. Guida, 30, Donaldson Street, Les Effort East, San Fernando, Trinidad, W.1.

UNITED KINGDOM: F. W. Passey, 59d Windmill Road, Headington, Oxford.

UNITED STATES OF AMERICA: Bryce E. Deloach, P.O. Box 575, Denville, N.J. 07834.

VENEZUELA: Andres Boulton, Apartado Postal 3623, Caracas, 101.

ZAMBIA: J. A. Richardson, P.O. Box 1608, Ndola.

Appendix B

ADDRESSES OF UFO JOURNALS MENTIONED

Flying Saucer Review, c/o Compendium Books, 281 Camden High Street, London, N.W.1.
Flying Saucer Review Case Histories, same address.
Flying Saucers, Amherst, Wisconsin, Wisconsin—54406, U.S.A.
Ondes Vives, 26 rue Louis-Blanc, 95 Saint-Leu-la-Foret, Val d'Oise, France.

References

INTRODUCTION

1. LE POER TRENCH, BRINSLEY, *The Flying Saucer Story*, Neville Spearman, London, 1966, p. 129. Ace Books, New York, 1969, pp. 119–20. Tandem, London, 1973, pp. 112–13.

2. SANDERSON, IVAN T., *Invisible Residents*, The World Publishing Company, Cleveland, Ohio, U.S.A., and Nelson, Foster & Scott Ltd., Canada, 1970.

3. GARDNER, MARSHALL B., *A Journey to the Earth's Interior*. Published by the author at Aurora, Illinois, 1920. Health Research, Mokelumne, California, 1964.

4. REED, WILLIAM, *The Phantom of the Poles*, Walter S. Rockey Company, New York, 1906. Health Research, Mokelumne, California, 1964.

CHAPTER 1

1. BRAGHINE, COLONEL A., *The Shadow of Atlantis*, Rider & Co., London, 1938, p. 14.

2. DONNELLY, IGNATIUS, *Atlantis: The Antediluvian World*, Samson Low, Marston & Co. Ltd., London, 1910, p. 3.

3. SPENCE, DR. LEWIS, *The Problem of Atlantis*, London, 1925, p. 25.

4. HULL, E., *The Sub-Oceanic Physiography of the North Atlantic*, London, 1912.

5. TERMIER, P., 'Atlantis', Bulletin de l'Institut Océanographique No. 256 (Paris), 1913.

6. TERMIER, P., 'Atlantis', Annual Report of the Smithsonian Institute for 1915. Washington, pp. 219–34.

7. SPENCE, DR. LEWIS, *The History of Atlantis*, London, 1925, pp. 57–8.

8. SCHARFF, R. F., 'Some Remarks on the Atlantis Problem'. Proceedings of Royal Irish Academy, Vol. 24.

9. SPENCE, DR. LEWIS, *The History of Atlantis*, p. 63.
10. WOLLASTON, T. V., *Testacea Atlantica*, London, 1878.
11. BRAGHINE, COLONEL A., *The Shadow of Atlantis*, pp. 79–81.

CHAPTER 2

1. SYKES, EGERTON. Special report to author.
2. WAY, APPIAN, (Comyns Beaumont). *The Riddle of the Earth*, Rider & Company, London, 1924, p. 229.
3. AELIAN, *Varia Hist.*, Vol. 3.
4. DONNELLY, IGNATIUS, *Atlantis: The Antediluvian World*, Samson Low, Marston & Co. Ltd., London, 1910, p. 284.
5. —, p. 285.
6. —, p. 286.
7. —, p. 287.
8. BRAGHINE, COLONEL A., *The Shadow of Atlantis*, p. 25.
9. KOLOSIMO, PETER, *Timeless Earth*, The Garnstone Press, London, 1973, p. 141.
10. Ibid.
11. WILKINS, HAROLD T., *Mysteries of Ancient South America*, Rider & Co., London, 1946, p. 24 footnote.
12. BRAGHINE, COLONEL A., *The Shadow of Atlantis*, pp. 31–2.

CHAPTER 3

1. HAPGOOD, CHARLES H., *Maps of the Ancient Sea Kings – Evidence of Advanced Civilization in the Ice Age!*, Chilton Company, Philadelphia, 1966, p. 2.

CHAPTER 4

1. MARKHAM, SIR CLEMENS, *The Incas of Peru*, London, 1910, p. 21.
2. —, p. 23.
3. —, p. 23.
4. POSNANSKY, A., *Tiahuanaco: The Cradle of American Man*, La Paz., 1946, pp. 15 & 39.
5. LE POER TRENCH, BRINSLEY, *Men Among Mankind*,

Neville Spearman, London, 1962, p. 21. Fontana Paperbacks, London, 1973, under title of *Temple of the Stars*, p. 21.

6. VELIKOVSKY, IMMANUEL, *Worlds in Collision*, Gollancz, London, 1950. Macmillan, New York, and Doubleday, New York.

7. FAWCETT, H. P., *Exploration Fawcett: the Travel Diaries & Notes of Colonel H. P. Fawcett*, edited by B. Fawcett, London, 1953.

8. WILKINS, HAROLD T., *Mysteries of Ancient South America*, p. 190.

9. BELLAMY, H. S., *Built Before The Flood: The Problem of the Tiahuanaco Ruins*, London, 1947, pp. 42–3.

10. —, p. 50.

11. VERRILL, A. H. and E. R., *America's Ancient Civilizations*, New York, 1953, p. 204.

12. SQUIER, E. G., *Peru, Incidents of Travel and Exploration in the Land of the Incas*, 2nd edition, New York, 1878, p. 279. The 1st edition appeared in 1847.

13. LE POER TRENCH, BRINSLEY, *Men Among Mankind*, pp. 21–2. *Temple of the Stars*, p. 22.

14. HEYERDAHL, THOR, *American Indians in the Pacific*, London and Stockholm, 1952, p. 387.

15. LE POER TRENCH, BRINSLEY, *Men Among Mankind*, p. 24. *Temple of the Stars*, pp. 24–5.

16. —, *Men Among Mankind*, pp. 26–7. *Temple of the Stars*, pp. 27–8.

CHAPTER 5

1. GUERBER, H. A., *The Myths of Greece and Rome*, George G. Harrap & Co. Ltd., London, 1953. Printing of new revised edition, 1938, pp. 14–15. First edition, 1907.

2. *Larousse Encyclopaedia of Mythology*, Batchworth Press, London, 1959, p. 97.

CHAPTER 6

1. VON DANIKEN, ERICH, *The Gold of the Gods*, Souvenir Press, London, 1973, p. 1.

2. —, p. 60.

3. —, p. 181.

4. —, p. 181.

5. KOLOSIMO, PETER, *Timeless Earth*, p. 40.

6. WILKINS, HAROLD T., *Mysteries of Ancient South America*, pp. 169–70.

7. —, pp. 175–6.

8. KOLOSIMO, PETER, *Timeless Earth*, p. 40.

9. Ibid.

10. WILKINS, HAROLD T., *Mysteries of Ancient South America*, p. 174.

11. KOLOSIMO, PETER, *Timeless Earth*, p. 70.

12. —, p. 71.

13. Ibid.

CHAPTER 7

1. LE POER TRENCH, BRINSLEY, *Men Among Mankind*, p. 31. *Temple of the Stars*, p. 33.

2. BRAGHINE, COLONEL A., *The Shadow of Atlantis*, p. 17.

3. BANCROFT, H. H., *The Native Races of the Pacific States of North America*, in 5 volumes. See Vols. 3 & 5, 1875–6.

4. PURCHAS, SAMUEL, *A Treatize on Brazil, written by a Portugall*, which had long lived there: in Book 7, Chapter 1, Vol. 16 of *Hakluytus Posthumus, or Purchas His Pilgrimes, Contayning a History of the World in Sea Voyages and Lande Travels by Englishmen and Others*, 20 vols., Glasgow, MCMVI.

5. ROSE, H. J., *Handbook of Greek Mythology, including its Extension to Rome*, London, 1928, p. 218.

6. BRAGHINE, COLONEL A., *The Shadow of Atlantis*, p. 151.

7. BELLAMY, H. S., *Moons, Myths and Man: A Reinterpretation*, London, 1936, p. 95.

8. Ibid.

9. —, p. 96.

10. FLINT, R. F., *Glacial Geology and the Pleistocene Epoch*, New York, 1947.

11. BELLAMY, H. S., *Moons, Myths and Man: A Reinterpretation*, p. 97.

12. DONNELLY, IGNATIUS, *Ragnarok: The Age of Fire and Gravel*, D. Appleton and Company, New York, 1883, p. 135.

13. MOTTRAM, R. H., *Noah*, London, 1937, p. 28.

14. —, p. 41.

15. CHADBOURNE, M., *Anahuac: A Tale of a Mexican Journey*, London, 1954, p. 84.

16. GAMBOA, S. DE, *History of the Incas*, Hakluyt Society, Ser. 11. Vol. xxii (Cambridge), 1907, p. 32.

17. DENIS, M. F., *Une Fête Brasilienne Célébré à Rouen en 1550*, 1550, p. 82.

18. MARTINIUS, P. M. DE, *History of China*, Vol. 1, p. 12.

19. HOWORTH, H. H., *The Mammoth and the Flood*, London, 1887, pp. 462–3.

CHAPTER 8

1. WILKINS, HAROLD T., *Secret Cities of Old South America*, Rider & Company, London, 1950, p. 433.

2. GUERBER, H. E., *The Myths of Greece and Rome*, p. 95.

3. *Encyclopaedia Britannica, The*, Eleventh edition, Vol. 7, p. 815.

CHAPTER 9

1. LE POER TRENCH, BRINSLEY, *The Sky People*, Neville Spearman, London, 1960. Award Books, New York, 1970. Edition J'ai Lu, Paris, 1970. Tandem, London, 1971.

2. WARREN, WILLIAM F., *Paradise Found, or The Cradle of the Human Race at the North Pole*, Houghton, Nifflin and Company, Boston, 1885, p. 240 quoting from *Records of the Past*. Translated by the Rev. A. H. Sayce.

3. PALMER, RAYMOND A., 'What the Bible says about the Polar Mystery Area'. *Flying Saucers*, August, 1960.

4. CHARROUX, ROBERT, *The Mysterious Unknown*, Robert Lafont, Paris, 1969. Neville Spearman, London, 1972.

CHAPTER 10

1. REED, WILLIAM, *The Phantom of the Poles*, Health Research edition, pp. 30–1.

2. GARDNER, MARSHALL B., *A Journey to the Earth's Interior*, Health Research edition, p. 85.

3. PALMER, RAYMOND A., 'Saucers from Earth!' *Flying Saucers*, December, 1959. And, O'Brien, Brian J., 'Radiation Belts', *Scientific American*, May, 1963.

4. MICHEL, AIMÉ, *Flying Saucers and the Straight-Line Mystery*, Criterion Books, New York, 1958.

5. Letter to author from The Institute of Geological Sciences, Exhibition Road, London, S.W.7 enclosing photostat material about the structure of the Earth.

6. GARDNER, MARSHALL B., *A Journey to the Earth's Interior*, Health Research edition. Reference caption opposite p. 62 in that book.

CHAPTER 11

1. NANSEN, DR. FRIDTJOF, *Farthest North: Being the Record of a Voyage of Exploration of the Ship Fram 1893–1896 and of a Fifteen months Sleigh Journey by Dr. Nansen and Lieut. Johnson.* 2 Volumes, Harper & Brothers, London and New York, 1898.

2. —, Vol. 2, pp. 18–19.

3. GARDNER, MARSHALL B., *A Journey to the Earth's Interior*, Health Research edition, p. 301.

4. —, pp. 301–302.

5. —, p. 302, quoting from another book by Dr. Nansen, *In Northern Mists*, Vol. 2, William Heinemann, London, 1911.

6. *Encyclopaedia Britannica, The*, eleventh edition, Vol. 21, pp. 30–1.

7. GARDNER, MARSHALL B., p. 193.

CHAPTER 12

1. Gordienko, P. A., 'The Arctic Ocean', *Scientific American*, May, 1961.

2. PALMER, RAYMOND A., 'The North Pole – Russian Style', *Flying Saucers*, March, 1962.

CHAPTER 13

1. *National Geographic*, July, 1959.
2. PALMER, RAYMOND A., Editorial, *Flying Saucers*, August, 1960.

CHAPTER 14

1. REED, WILLIAM, *The Phantom of the Poles*, Health Research edition, p. 126.
2. Ibid.
3. —, p. 210, also quoting from E. K. Kane's work, *Arctic Explorations in Search of Sir John Franklin 1853–55*, J. B. Lippincott & Company, Philadelphia, 1856.
4. —, p. 23.
5. —, p. 175, quoting from *Captain Hall's Last Trip* (author and publisher not given).
6. GREELY, A. W., *Three Years of Arctic Service*, Charles Scribner's Sons, New York, 1886.

CHAPTER 15

1. PALMER, RAYMOND A., 'Earth's Centre of Gravity – Up or Down?' *Flying Saucers*, December, 1959.

CHAPTER 16

1. *Encyclopaedia Britannica, The*, fourteenth edition, 1967 printing, Vol. 4, p. 507.
2. PALMER, RAYMOND A., 'Saucers from Earth!', *Flying Saucers*, December, 1959.
3. GIANNINI, F. AMEDO, *Worlds Beyond the Poles*, Vantage Press, New York, 1959.
4. PALMER, RAYMOND A., reply to a reader's letter, *Flying Saucers*, September, 1970.
5. GRAFFLIN, MISS DOROTHY E., a letter published in *Flying Saucers*, September, 1970.

6. REVIS, MR. BILL G., extract from a letter published in *Flying Saucers*, March 1971.

CHAPTER 17

1. ARNOLD, KENNETH, and PALMER, RAY, *The Coming of the Saucers*, privately published by the authors at Boise, Idaho and Amherst, Wisconsin, 1952, p. 132.
2. CREIGHTON, GORDON W., 'A Cigar-Shaped UFO over Antarctica', *Flying Saucer Review*, Vol. 14, No. 2 (March–April, 1968).
3. LLOYD, DAN, 'Things are hotting up in the Arctic', *Flying Saucer Review*, Vol. 11, No. 5 (September–October, 1965).
4. PALMER, RAYMOND A., editorial, *Flying Saucers*, March, 1971.

CHAPTER 18

1. PALMER, RAYMOND A., editorial, *Flying Saucers*, June, 1970.

CHAPTER 19

1. PALMER, RAYMOND A., editorial, *Flying Saucers*, Summer, 1973, Issue No. 81.

CHAPTER 20

1. WILKINS, HAROLD T., *Flying Saucers Uncensored*, The Citadel Press, New York, 1955, pp. 97–8.

CHAPTER 21

1. PALMER, RAY, 'Invitation to Adventure', from the book by Richard S. Shaver: *The Hidden World*, Palmer Publications, Amherst, Wisconsin, 1961, p. 10–11.

2. VERNE, JULES, *Journey to the Centre of the Earth*, originally published in France 1864.

3. EMERSON, WILLIAM GEORGE, *The Smoky God*, Palmer Publications, Amherst, Wisconsin, 1965.

4. TOLKIEN, PROFESSOR J. R. R., *The Lord of the Rings*, George Allen and Unwin, London, 1968.

CHAPTER 22

1. LE POER TRENCH, BRINSLEY, *The Eternal Subject*, Souvenir Press, London, 1973. Stein and Day, New York, 1973, and Pan Books, London, 1974. Both under the title of *Mysterious Visitors*.

2. KEEL, JOHN A., 'The UFO evidence everyone ignores', *Saga*, June, 1973.

CHAPTER 23

1. RUPPELT, EDWARD J., *The Report on Unidentified Flying Objects*, Doubleday & Company, Garden City, New York, 1956. pp. 41–5.

2. ARNOLD, KENNETH, and PALMER, RAY, *The Coming of the Saucers*, p. 31.

3. SIEGMOND, WARREN, 'Let's Talk Space', *Flying Saucer Review*, Vol. 1, No. 3 (July–August, 1955).

4. BARKER, GRAY, *They Knew Too Much About Flying Saucers*, New York, 1956, p. 132.

5. KEEL, JOHN A., 'The UFO evidence everyone ignores', *Saga*, June, 1973.

6. SALEMI, J. C., 'L'Aventure de J. M.', *Ondes Vives*, August, 1973, quoting from the journal *Hebdo*, of 31 March, 1973.

CHAPTER 24

1. WILKINS, HAROLD T., *Flying Saucers Uncensored*, pp. 157–8.

CHAPTER 25

1. KEEL, JOHN A., *Strange Creatures from Time and Space*, Fawcett Publications, Greenwich, Connecticut, p. 64.
2. Puma Research Group, The, 83 Golden Grove, Bevios, Southampton, Hampshire.
3. BOWEN, CHARLES, 'Mystery Animals', *Flying Saucer Review*, Vol. 10, No. 6 (November–December, 1964).
4. *Flying Saucer Review*, 'World Round Up' feature in following issues: Vol. 11, No. 2 (March–April, 1965), pp. 24–5; Vol. 12, No. 5 (September–October, 1966), p. 28; Vol. 15, No. 5 September–October, 1969), p. 36; Vol. 16, No. 6 (November–December, 1970), p. 29; Vol. 17, No. 3 (May–June, 1971), cover iii; Vol. 17, No. 5 (September– October, 1971), p. 31.
5. *Flying Saucer Review*, 'The Socorro Classic', Vol. 10, No. 6 (November–December, 1964), reprinted from the *UFO Investigator*, July–August, 1964 (the bulletin of the National Investigations Committee on Aerial Phenomena, NICAP).
6. CLARK, JEROME, and COLEMAN, LOREN, 'On the Trail of Pumas, Panthers and ULAs', *Fate*, June and July, 1972.

CHAPTER 26

1. LE POER TRENCH, BRINSLEY, *The Eternal Subject*, pp. 17, 95–100, 102, 107, 109, 111–112.
2. RIBERA, ANTONIO, letter to author, April, 1967.
3. KEEL, JOHN A., *Operation Trojan Horse*, Souvenir Press, London, 1971, pp. 68, 73, 102–3, 201, 247, 249, 251, 271, 281, 296–7, 302–3.
4. WILKINS, HAROLD T., *Flying Saucers Uncensored*, pp. 129–30.

CHAPTER 27

1. KEEL, JOHN A., *Strange Creatures from Time and Space*, p. 274.
2. FREIXEDO, SALVADOR, 'UFOs over the Caribbean', *Flying Saucer Review Case Histories*, April, 1973 (sister publication to *Flying Saucer Review*).

CHAPTER 28

1. KEEL, JOHN A., *Our Haunted Planet*, Fawcett Publications, Greenwich, Connecticut, 1971, p. 217.
2. LE POER TRENCH, BRINSLEY, *Operation Earth*, Neville Spearman, London, 1969, pp. 106–9. Tandem, London, 1974.
3. —, *Men Among Mankind*, pp. 58–9.
4. HOYLE, SIR FRED, *Of Men and Galaxies*, Heinemann, London, 1965, p. 47.

CHAPTER 29

1. WILKINS, HAROLD T., *Flying Saucers Uncensored*, p. 71.

CHAPTER 30

1. STEARN, JESS, *The Door to the Future*, Frederick Muller, London, 1964, p. 314.

CHAPTER 31

1. *National Enquirer*, Lantana, Florida, 16 December, 1973.
2. DE CHARDIN, PIERRE TEILHARD, *The Future of Man*, William Collins, London, pp. 276ff.

Index

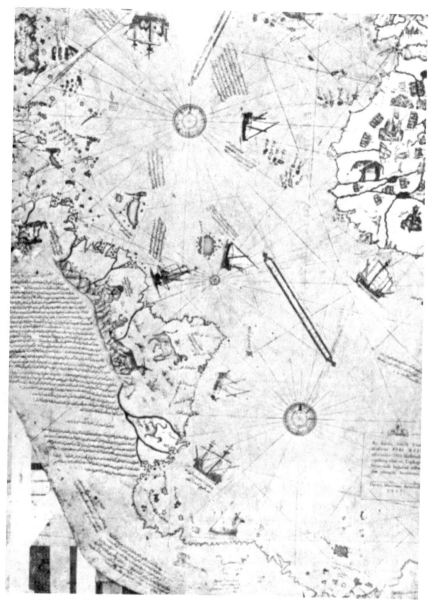

Plate 1. The fabulous Piri Re'is Map
Photograph: Library of Congress, Washington, D.C.

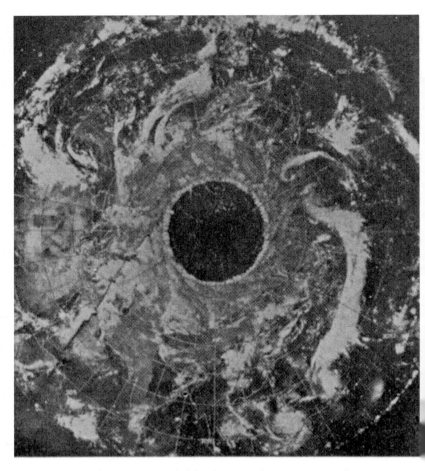

Plate 2. The most remarkable photograph ever. It was taken by
ESSA-7 satellite on 23 November, 1968. There is almost no cloud
cover; the ice fields on the surface can be observed, and the hole
at the North Pole can be clearly seen.

Photograph: courtesy *Flying Saucers* magazine and Environmental
Science Administration, U.S. Department of Commerce.

Plate 3. Photograph taken by same satellite ESSA-7 on same day,
23 November, 1968, showing cloud cover over South Pole.

Photograph: courtesy *Flying Saucers* magazine and Environmental
Science Administration, U.S. Department of Commerce.

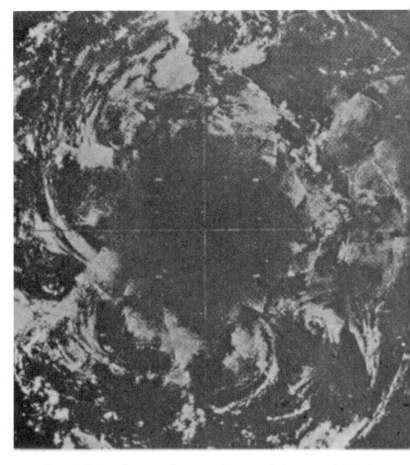

Plate 4. This photograph was taken on 6 January, 1967, by satellite ESSA-3, clearly showing the hole at the North Pole.

Photograph: courtesy *Flying Saucers* magazine and Environmental Science Administration, U.S. Department of Commerce.

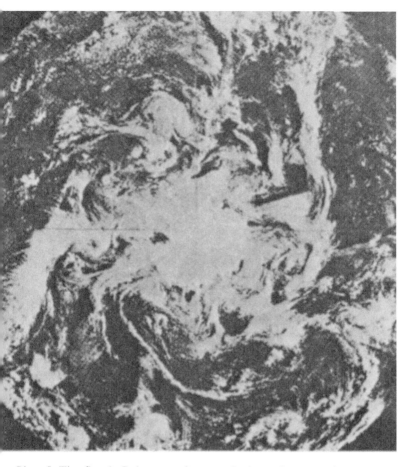

Plate 5. The South Pole area photographed on the same day, 6 January, 1967, by ESSA-3, showing ice cap cloud cover.

Photograph: courtesy *Flying Saucers* magazine and Environmental Science Administration, U.S. Department of Commerce.

Plate 6. This photograph of the Earth was taken with the ATS-111 satellite camera from a height of 23,000 miles. Note what looks like a 'moon crater' at top of picture. This could be the lip of the hole from another angle.

Photograph: courtesy *Flying Saucers* magazine and the National Aeronautics and Space Administration Book *Exploring Space with a Camera*.

Plate 7. This is ATS-111's photograph of the Earth taken on 18 November, 1967. Once again this strange depression can be seen at the top of the picture.

Photograph: courtesy *Flying Saucers* magazine and the National Aeronautics and Space Administration Book *Exploring Space with a Camera*.

Plate 8. UFO photographed over Faymonville, province of Liege, Belgium, on 19 July, 1972, by M. Mathar.
Photograph: courtesy of SOBEPS.

Plate 9. Another photograph of the same UFO over Faymonville showing more detail.
Photograph: courtesy of SOBEPS.

Printed in Great Britain
by Amazon

24048764R00126